D0357170

AMERICAN ATTITUDES
TOWARD JAPAN,
1941-1975

LIBRARY
ARAPAHOE COMMUNITY COLLEGE
5900 SOUTH SANTA FE
LITTLETON, COLORADO 80120
MAY 1 - 19

AEI-Hoover
policy studies

The studies in this series are issued jointly
by the American Enterprise Institute
for Public Policy Research and the Hoover
Institution on War, Revolution and Peace.
They are designed to focus on
policy problems of current and future interest,
to set forth the factors underlying
these problems and to evaluate
courses of action available to policy makers.
The views expressed in these studies
are those of the authors and do not necessarily
reflect the views of the staff, officers
or members of the governing boards of
AEI or the Hoover Institution.

AMERICAN ATTITUDES TOWARD JAPAN, 1941-1975

Sheila K. Johnson

American Enterprise Institute for Public Policy Research
Washington, D. C.

Hoover Institution on War, Revolution and Peace
Stanford University, Stanford, California

AEI-Hoover Policy Study 15, November 1975
(Hoover Institution Studies 51)

ISBN 0-8447-3179-X

Library of Congress Catalog Card No. 75-24845

© 1975 by American Enterprise Institute for Public Policy Research
Washington, D. C. Permission to quote from or to reproduce materials
in this publication is granted when due acknowledgment is made.

Printed in the United States of America

Acknowledgments

Since I cannot claim to be a "Japan specialist," but am merely an anthropologist who has lived in, and read about, Japan, this study owes much to the encouragement of two scholars whose credentials far exceed mine. Professor Donald C. Hellmann is responsible for suggesting the topic to me, as well as for sponsoring its publication. Professor Chalmers Johnson, who first awakened my interest in Japan by taking me there, gave me good advice throughout the research and writing of these pages. In addition, Chapters 1 and 3 were circulated at a meeting of the California Arms Control and Foreign Policy Seminar, which took place 5–8 January 1975, in Palm Springs, California, where I benefited from the comments of a number of knowledgeable scholars. Needless to say, no one but myself is to blame for any deficiencies of fact and judgment that may remain.

Contents

1
The Ambiguous Legacy

It seems that Americans have always been ambivalent about Japan. Commodore Perry's men found the Japanese to be "the most polite people on earth"; yet Perry was deeply frustrated by what he considered to be their outright lies, evasions, and hypocrisy. As Foster Rhea Dulles has commented, this bifurcate impression—of courtesy and hypocrisy— "helped to set a pattern of American thinking about the Japanese that has persisted for a century." [1] Lafcadio Hearn, one of the great romantic boosters of all that was Japanese, nevertheless lamented in a private letter: "But with what hideous rapidity Japan is modernizing, after all!— not in costume, or architecture, or habit, but in heart and manner. The emotional nature of the race is changing. Will it ever become beautiful again? Or failing to become attractive, can it ever become sufficiently complex to make a harmony with the emotional character of the West?" [2] Hearn also knew the cost of the old character and society, whose passing he lamented: "The old kindliness and grace of manners need not cease to charm us because we know that such manners were cultivated, for a thousand years, under the edge of the sword. . . . And this immemorial doctrine of filial piety, —exacting all that is noble, not less than all that is terrible, in duty, in gratitude, in self-denial. . . ." [3] In still a different mood, he reflected on the comment of another foreigner, a friend, who had said to him, "If those people [the Japanese] could only feel for us

---

[1] Foster Rhea Dulles, *Yankees and Samurai* (New York: Harper and Row, 1965), pp. 68-69.
[2] Elizabeth Stevenson, *Lafcadio Hearn* (New York: The Macmillan Co., 1961), p. 256.
[3] Lafcadio Hearn, *Japan: An Attempt at Interpretation* (New York: Macmillan, 1924 [copyright 1904]), pp. 502, 503.

1

the sympathy we feel toward them!" "Indeed," noted Hearn, "the whole question of life in Japan to a sensitive westerner was summed up in that half-utterance. The unspeakable absence of sympathy, as a result, perhaps, of all absence of comprehension, is a veritable torture." [4]

These early comments and thoughts reveal a great jumble of ambivalent feelings that has certainly not lessened during the last thirty-five years of American contact with Japan. The war, followed by the occupation, followed by a period of expanding tourism and trade, followed by a period of inflation and international instability marked by mutual recriminations between the two countries—all these have left their imprint on American attitudes. When a college class was recently asked to free-associate about Japan—to complete the sentence "When I think of Japan, I think of . . ."—the words that tumbled out included: small, fierce country; transistors; Hiroshima; geisha girls; beautiful trees and topography; Tokyo and traffic jams; kimonos; high degree of industrialization. And they tumbled out in no particular combinations: that is, a person who mentioned the tea ceremony might also mention transistor radios and cars, and someone who thought of brush-stroke painting might also think of kamikaze. When asked to name three prominent Japanese, from either the past or present, the students most frequently mentioned Tojo, Emperor Hirohito, and Prime Minister Tanaka; but some students thought of Bashō, Toshiro Mifune, and Kenzo Tange.

The sociologist Nathan Glazer has suggested that responses of this sort reveal two things: first, that American attitudes toward Japan are, in fact, quite shallow—that most Americans do not think much about Japan at all, and that their impressions are therefore likely to be hasty and contradictory; and second, that their ambivalence is an accurate reflection of the paradoxical nature of Japan and the Japanese—that, in the words of Ruth Benedict,

> The Japanese are, to the highest degree, both aggressive and unaggressive, both militaristic and aesthetic, both insolent and polite, rigid and adaptable, submissive and resentful of being pushed around, loyal and treacherous, brave and timid, conservative and hospitable to new ways. They are terribly concerned about what other people will think of their behavior, and they are also overcome by guilt when other people know nothing of their misstep. Their soldiers are disciplined to the hilt but are also insubordinate.[5]

---

[4] Stevenson, *Lafcadio Hearn,* p. 268.

[5] Nathan Glazer, "From Ruth Benedict to Herman Kahn: The Postwar Japanese

I do not happen to think that either of Glazer's contentions about the origins of American attitudes is precisely accurate. American perceptions of Japan strike me as no more shallow than American perceptions of France, Spain, or Russia. In fact, they may be more profound, since they tend to be based on wartime experiences, tourism, or contact with Japanese products, from movies to automobiles. (What words would the average American associate with Spain, for example, and what prominent Spaniards might he name other than Franco?) Neither do I think that Japanese character is so inherently contradictory that it necessarily elicits an ambivalent response. Japanese character is quite different in certain respects from American character, and this difference may simultaneously attract and repel Americans. But this is not at all the same thing as saying that the Japanese character harbors such a galaxy of traits that one can only respond with confusion.

Another possible explanation for American ambivalence toward Japan is a simple situational one. Most middle-aged Americans have experienced during their lifetimes a whole range of attitudes toward Japan called forth in succession by changing historical situations: rage and fear during World War II, pity and compassion during the occupation, admiration and curiosity during the late 1950s and early 1960s, annoyance and perhaps a measure of envy during the late 1960s and early 1970s. None of these feelings, however, has entirely superseded the preceding ones; instead they overlie one another in the complex pattern we see today. Nor does any one individual or social group in America display the entire range of feelings toward Japan. An individual's feelings will be influenced by his age, sex, political persuasion, education, and the nature of his or her contact with Japan. This diversity of opinion also tends to register on questionnaires and surveys as ambivalence.

Nevertheless, the question of whether there is a relationship between Japanese national character and American perceptions of Japan and the Japanese is an important one that cannot be lightly dismissed. All studies of prejudice and national stereotyping must at some point deal with the "kernel of truth" hypothesis—the notion that underneath all the psychological and social reasons why one group of people may

Image in the American Mind," forthcoming in Akira Iriye, ed., *Mutual Images: Essays in American-Japanese Relations* (Cambridge, Mass.: Harvard University Press, 1975), and Ruth Benedict, *The Chrysanthemum and the Sword* (Boston: Houghton Mifflin Co., 1946), pp. 2-3.

call another ethnic group lazy, dirty, musical, greedy, or sly, there is a basis in fact. During World War II, Americans perceived Japanese as sneaky, cruel, and fanatical; had anyone had the temerity to ask *why* they felt this way, the answer would have been obvious: because the Japanese *are* sneaky, cruel, and fanatical. Today, many Americans think of the Japanese as artistic, industrious, and reserved, and these same Americans would no doubt be prepared to defend their opinions by citing evidence that the Japanese are, in fact, all of these things. Those who are disturbed by the disparity between our wartime and present-day opinions are merely told that the Japanese have changed— that losing the war and being forced to become democratic during the occupation did them a world of good. Unfortunately, there is no evidence that the Japanese temperament has changed radically. The considered opinion of most psychologists, anthropologists, and sociologists is that prewar and postwar Japanese share certain recognizable characteristics—call it "national character," if you will—and that wartime studies merely emphasized the dark characteristics, whereas postwar studies have tended to be more flattering.

Wartime National Character Studies

It is an unfortunate fact that the entire field of national character studies—or "studies of cultures at a distance," as they were sometimes called—began as an adjunct of World War II. To be sure, the intellectual roots of such studies lie in the 1920s and 1930s, when Freudianism had a profound impact on American anthropology and when a number of anthropologists began administering psychological tests in primitive societies and applying psychoanalytic interpretations to some of their cultural data. However, with the start of World War II, many of these same scholars went to work for the Office of War Information or other branches of the government, where they began applying their techniques not merely to complex societies but to societies with which the United States was then at war. The practical purposes of these studies were to discover what might break the morale of the German or Japanese soldier, what sort of propaganda might work best among the occupied nations of Europe and Southeast Asia, and what sort of occupation policies the United States should implement once it had won the war.

4

In the case of Japan, most of the anthropologists and psychologists who set out to delineate her social and character structure had never been to Japan, could neither read nor speak Japanese, and had no deep prior acquaintance with her history or culture. This list would include Geoffrey Gorer, Gregory Bateson, Margaret Mead, Ruth Benedict, Weston LaBarre, Alexander Leighton, and Morris Opler. Two exceptions were Douglas Haring, an anthropologist who had lived in Japan from 1917 to 1922 and again from 1924 to 1926, and John Embree, an anthropologist who had married an American woman born and raised in Japan and who, from mid-1935 to late-1936, lived in a small Kyushu village about which he wrote a village study that is still considered a classic.[6]

It would be wrong to imply that the differences that developed among these scholars—and the differences that a present-day reader sees in their work—can be explained entirely in terms of the intuitive, "deeper" knowledge of the old Japan-hand versus the more schematic, perhaps superficial knowledge of the armchair scholar. One of the most sensitive, still highly regarded works to come out of these wartime efforts was Ruth Benedict's *The Chrysanthemum and the Sword*—based entirely on her reading of novels and secondary sources, her viewing of Japanese movies, and her interviews with Issei and Nisei. But Ruth Benedict was a special sort of scholar—a woman who was also a poet, who came to academic life late, and who in all her work revealed a gentle and perceptive judgment. But not all of those who were studying Japan from a distance, in the midst of a bitter war, were similarly endowed. Thus the basic analysis of Japanese character came to rest on the notion that harsh toilet training and an emphasis on shame rather than guilt had produced a nation of individuals who were obsessively clean, polite, and obsequious, but that "behind the rituals of the individual obsessive can always be discovered a deeply hidden, unconscious and extremely strong desire to be aggressive" and that "the sanctions for correct behavior in a Japanese environment would be no longer operative in a different environment and under different circumstances; and consequently all the aggression and cruelty which is unsuitable in Japanese contexts can be allowed vent."[7]

---

[6] John Embree, *Suye Mura: A Japanese Village* (Chicago: University of Chicago Press, 1939).

[7] Geoffrey Gorer, "Themes in Japanese Culture," The New York Academy of Sciences *Transactions,* series 2, vol. 5, no. 5 (March 1943), pp. 119, 118.

In a postwar article, John Embree protested that a number of the childhood training practices on which such national character analyses were based, were practices he had never observed during the course of his fieldwork in Japan. He went on to argue that "In much of the character structure writing about the Japanese there is an ethnocentrism which fitted in well with the social needs of the war period during which the 'scientific' conclusions as to their character were made. Racist interpretations were socially as well as scientifically unacceptable at this time but 'character structure' interpretations were all right and served just as well in the literate world to 'explain' the international and domestic behavior of Japan."[8]

Douglas Haring, also writing after the war, suggested that much of the behavior that Gorer and others called "compulsive" and blamed on harsh toilet training could be better explained in terms of Japanese history. Haring argued that the Japanese had lived, since the beginning of the Tokugawa period (1603), under a form of government that stressed strict sumptuary laws and correct social behavior, enforced by an efficient network of political spies and samurai. (This is a point also made by Lafcadio Hearn.) In the period extending from 1868 to 1945, the samurai were replaced with a centralized police force, but the average Japanese reacted in the same, learned way: "All the features of the alleged 'compulsive personality' of the Japanese are logical fruits of the police state. An explanation centered in diapers is suspect if it neglects three centuries of fear-inspired discipline. To say this does not refute psychoanalytic interpretations, for relentless police supervision modifies the human psyche profoundly. . . . Police controls impose strains on individuals—strains that multiply and become more rigorous as adulthood is reached."[9]

The great virtue of the Embree-Haring approach is that it frees us of some of the wartime biases of national character studies without throwing out the baby with the bathwater—that is, without denying that our perceptions of the Japanese may have some basis in reality. As Embree has pointed out: "A summary (even when accurate) of a nation's citizens' behavior traits, while of some value in predicting individual behavior of members of the society, does not provide a magic

[8] John Embree, "Standard Error and Japanese Character: A Note on Political Interpretation," *World Politics,* vol. 2, no. 3 (April 1950), p. 442.

[9] Douglas Haring, "Japanese National Character: Cultural Anthropology, Psychoanalysis, and History," *Yale Review,* Spring 1953, p. 386.

explanation for a nation's aggressive warfare, whether it be Japanese, British, American, or Russian."[10] We should therefore be able to look at some of our reactions to the Japanese during the war, and later on, without constant reference to what may or may not be their basic personality. If we do that, it will become clear, I think, that many of our reactions are situational—they are responses to immediate acts and circumstances—and that where we are reacting to the Japanese qua Japanese we are, often as not, reacting merely in terms of how different they are from ourselves. For example, the Japanese are generally speaking more reserved than Americans—a national character trait that may strike us as either politeness or aloofness, depending on how favorably disposed we happen to be at the time—but the fact that we react to this quality of reserve is probably conditioned by our own less formal style of behavior.

The Migrating Stereotype

There is one other ingredient of American perceptions of the Japanese, and this is our concurrent perceptions of the Chinese. Since both nations are "Oriental" and therefore somewhat strange to Americans, superficial similarities have sometimes led to a sort of ideological lumping together of the two. One study of wartime American attitudes toward Japanese-Americans argues that in part the Japanese-Americans simply inherited the prejudices that had built up against Chinese immigrants during an earlier period:

> One popular method [of transferring this prejudice] was to attribute to the Japanese all the alleged crimes of the Chinese by emphasizing their similarities—and then to point out their differences as compounding the felony. Thus the United States Industrial Commission reported in 1901 that the Japanese "are more servile than the Chinese, but less obedient and far less desirable. They have most of the vices of the Chinese, with none of the virtues. They underbid the Chinese in everything, and are as a class tricky, unreliable and dishonest."[11]

A more disturbing tendency in recent times has been the development of two polar-opposite stereotypes about Orientals, which can be

---

[10] Embree, "Standard Error," p. 443.

[11] Jacobus TenBroek, Edward N. Barnhart, and Floyd W. Matson, *Prejudice, War and the Constitution* (Berkeley: University of California Press, 1954), p. 23.

pasted like labels onto either the Japanese or the Chinese, as the occasion warrants. The favorable Oriental stereotype includes such attributes as patience, cleanliness, courtesy, and the ability to work hard; the unfavorable one emphasizes clannishness, silent contempt, sneakiness, and cruelty. There is a good deal of casual evidence that these two stereotypes alternate between the Japanese and the Chinese, and that when one nation is being viewed in the light of the favorable stereotype, the other will be saddled with the unfavorable epithets. An example of the blanket "Oriental" stereotype, combined with the denigration of the Japanese as opposed to the Chinese, can be found in *Time* magazine's wartime instructions to its readers explaining "How to tell your friends from the Japs."

Scholars working on national character studies during World War II were not immune to such polarized views. The psychologically oriented anthropologist Weston LaBarre wrote two important papers setting forth "Some Observations on Character Structure in the Orient"—one dealing with the Chinese, among whom he had spent some two years as a liaison officer attached to General Stilwell's headquarters, and the other dealing with the Japanese. He began his paper on the Chinese by confessing, "It is nearly impossible for an American who has first-hand acquaintance with the Chinese not to develop for them and for their civilization an affection and a profound respect"; he then proceeded to assert that "despite all provocations and all their many wars, the Chinese have never become militaristic," and "the Chinese are not imperialistic . . . [they] have never had the evangelical impulse to carry their values to other peoples and to impose these upon others by conquest." Moreover, "Americans and Chinese are alike in their fundamental extroversion," and "American and Chinese civilizations are natural and inevitable allies." Not surprisingly, LaBarre found the Japanese to be compulsive, self-righteous, fanatical, arrogant, and suspicious.[12]

It goes without saying that a few years later one can find examples in which these stereotypes are completely reversed. The Chinese have become fanatical, cruel, and militaristic, whereas the Japanese have demonstrated themselves to be compliant, gentle, and peace-loving. Shortly after the Chinese entered the Korean War, General MacArthur,

---

[12] Weston LaBarre, "Some Observations on Character Structure in the Orient: The Japanese and The Chinese (Parts I and II)," *Psychiatry*, vol. 8, no. 3 (1945), pp. 319-42; vol. 9, no. 3 (1946), pp. 215-38; and vol. 9, no. 4 (1946), pp. 375-95.

Chinese   *Japanese*

HOW TO TELL YOUR FRIENDS FROM THE JAPS

Of these four faces of young men *(above)* and middle-aged men *(below)* the two on the left are Chinese, the two on the right Japanese. There is no infallible way of telling them apart, because the same racial strains are mixed in both. Even an anthropologist, with calipers and plenty of time to measure heads, noses, shoulders, hips, is sometimes stumped. A few rules of thumb—not always reliable:

▶ Some Chinese are tall (average: 5 ft. 5 in.). Virtually all Japanese are short (average: 5 ft. 2½ in.).

▶ Japanese are likely to be stockier and broader-hipped than short Chinese.

▶ Japanese—except for wrestlers—are seldom fat; they often dry up and grow lean as they age. The Chinese often put on weight, particularly if they are prosperous (in China, with its frequent famines, being fat is esteemed as a sign of being a solid citizen).

▶ Chinese, not as hairy as Japanese, seldom grow an impressive mustache.

▶ Most Chinese avoid horn-rimmed spectacles.

▶ Although both have the typical epicanthic fold of the upper eyelid (which makes them look almond-eyed), Japanese eyes are usually set closer together.

▶ Those who know them best often rely on facial expression to tell them apart: the Chinese expression is likely to be more placid, kindly, open; the Japanese more positive, dogmatic, arrogant.

In Washington, last week, Correspondent Joseph Chiang made things much easier by pinning on his lapel a large badge reading "Chinese Reporter—NOT *Japanese*—Please."

▶ Some aristocratic Japanese have thin, aquiline noses, narrow faces and, except for their eyes, look like Caucasians.

▶ Japanese are hesitant, nervous in conversation, laugh loudly at the wrong time.

▶ Japanese walk stiffly, erect, hard-heeled. Chinese, more relaxed, have an easy gait, sometimes shuffle.

Chinese   *Japanese*

Reprinted with permission, from **TIME**, The Weekly Newsmagazine, © Time, Inc.

9

who only a few years before had praised the Chinese for their devotion to the cause of freedom, was telling Elizabeth Gray Vining, "I can't throw these educated, carefully nurtured [American] boys against hordes of coolies."[13] The notion that pro-Chinese attitudes correlate with anti-Japanese attitudes, and vice versa, has even been explicitly formulated on occasion: when Charles Poore reviewed John Hersey's *Hiroshima,* he tried to protect Hersey from still anti-Japanese Americans who might regard the book as too sympathetic to Japan: "John Hersey would be among the last to favor the Japanese. He happens to have been born in China, which gives him a natural dislike for the Japanese that goes back to his childhood days."[14]

The seesaw correlation of American attitudes toward Japan and China—when one is up the other is down—strikes me as indicative of the fact that fundamentally we are reacting to something Oriental, something different from ourselves, and that the particular coloration we attach to a given country is dictated by current political considerations or events of the recent past. For this reason, I consider it more productive to put aside the ultimate question of what the Japanese are or are not, and to look instead at what Americans have thought and felt about them over the past thirty-five years and what sorts of occurrences seem to have shaped those thoughts and feelings.

Approaches to the Study of Attitudes

There are a variety of ways to approach the study of attitudes, one of the most obvious being via the public opinion poll. Unfortunately, not many opinion polls in the United States have asked questions about Japan. The only one that does so regularly is an annual Gallup poll commissioned by the Japanese Foreign Ministry since 1955, which asks a representative sample of Americans whether or not they consider Japan a reliable ally. The answers over the years have ranged from a high of 55 percent who thought Japan was "untrustworthy" (in mid-1960, at the height of the riots against the Security Treaty) to a low of 31 percent only a year later. In late 1973, 36 percent of those polled considered Japan a trustworthy ally and 37 percent considered her untrustworthy; the remainder, perhaps wisely, had no opinion. The

---

[13] Elizabeth Gray Vining, *Windows for the Crown Prince* (New York: J. B. Lippincott, 1952), p. 315.
[14] *New York Times Book Review,* 10 November 1946, p. 56.

problem with such a survey is that it does not really tell us very much about American attitudes, not even with regard to the question asked, since every respondent defines for himself what he means by untrustworthy. Some are no doubt thinking back to World War II and consider Japan untrustworthy because they are fearful that she could go to war with us again; others perhaps regard Japan as a militarily weak and therefore untrustworthy ally in the event of a war with China or Russia and would prefer to see her rearm. And, whatever the reasoning behind the answers, attitudes on such a narrow issue represent only a small segment of the spectrum of American reactions to Japan.

Another approach to the study of attitudes is via the pronouncements of "opinion leaders." This is the approach taken by Nathan Glazer, who analyzes the writings of Ruth Benedict, Edwin Reischauer, Zbigniew Brzezinski, and Herman Kahn, in an effort to discover what sorts of informed impressions have shaped American thinking.[15] Unquestionably, the views of opinion leaders have an impact on a small elite—including, one would hope, government policy makers. To the extent that the opinion leaders have their ideas translated into policy—an example would be the wartime anthropologists' conclusion that the Japanese emperor should not be forced to abdicate or be tried as a war criminal—or widely disseminated via the popular media, they may also shape public opinion. But the route is very indirect, and it is by no means readily apparent which ideas and controversies shaking the academic world are going to gain wider currency. Glazer reports that Ruth Benedict's *The Chrysanthemum and the Sword,* considered a classic in its field, sold only 28,000 hardback copies (a high-priced paper edition was not published until 1967) between 1946 and 1971. This amounts to a sale of about 1,000 copies a year, many of them to people like Glazer and myself, who have a professional interest in Japan, anthropology, or both. However, one gains some sense of the impact of this book when one reads in Ian Fleming's *You Only Live Twice:*

> [Tiger Tanaka] has acquired an ON with regard to me. That's an obligation—almost as important in the Japanese way of life as "face." When you have an ON, you're not very happy until you've discharged it *hon*orably, if you'll pardon the bad pun. And if a man makes you a present of a salmon, you mustn't repay him with a shrimp. It's got to be with an equally large salmon—larger, if possible—so that then you've jumped

---

[15] Glazer, "From Ruth Benedict to Herman Kahn."

11

the man, and now he has an ON with regard to you, and you're quids in morally, socially, and spiritually—and the last one's the most important.[16]

It was passages such as this, transparently based on Ruth Benedict's book, that led me to a third approach to the study of popular attitudes: a survey not of what the elite reads but of what is read by the general public—popular magazines, newspapers, and those few books that "break out" of the confines of a narrow audience-appeal to become best sellers. In order to see what such an approach might yield, I began by compiling a list of all the books dealing with Japan that have appeared on the *New York Times* best-seller list for more than one week since 1941 (see Table 1). (The *New York Times* bases its list on sales figures in bookstores across the country.) Such a compilation reveals a good deal about popular American interest in and knowledge of Japan. For one thing, it reveals how pervasive and lasting has been the American preoccupation with the war in the Pacific. Best sellers about the Japanese and World War II began with John Hersey's *Men on Bataan* in 1942 and Richard Tregaskis's *Guadalcanal Diary* in 1943. But books about the war continued to be best sellers throughout the 1950s and 60s: They included Robert Theobald's *The Final Secret of Pearl Harbor* published in 1954; Walter Lord's *Day of Infamy,* also about Pearl Harbor, in 1957; "Pappy" Boyington's *Baa Baa Black Sheep,* an enormous best seller that sold approximately 100,000 copies during 1958–59; John Toland's *But Not in Shame,* a best seller in 1962; and Walter Lord's *Incredible Victory,* about the battle of Midway, which was a big best seller during late 1967 and early 1968. One could add to this recitation of popular books, popular movies such as *Bridge on the River Kwai* (1957) and *Tora! Tora! Tora!* (1970).

It was the evidence of continued interest in the Pacific war that first led me to suspect there might be certain "themes" in American attitudes toward Japan, themes that weave in and out of our responses but that are never entirely absent in any period. My original intention had been to treat American attitudes toward Japan chronologically—the war, the occupation, the late fifties, the "Reischauer years" (1961–66, when E. O. Reischauer was American ambassador to Japan), and the late sixties and early seventies. To a certain extent, of course, the themes that I have drawn from popular literature do emerge chronologically:

---

[16] Ian Fleming, *You Only Live Twice* (New York: The New American Library, 1965), p. 35.

Table 1
BEST SELLERS DEALING WITH JAPAN, 1942–1973

Year	Author/Title	Number of Weeks on List
1942	John Hersey, *Men on Bataan*	26 (approx.)
1943	Richard Tregaskis, *Guadalcanal Diary*	26 (approx.)
1944	Joseph Clark Grew, *Ten Years in Japan*	22
1946	John Hersey, *Hiroshima*	5
1948-49	Norman Mailer, *The Naked and the Dead*	62
1951	John Gunther, *The Riddle of MacArthur*	18
1952	Elizabeth Gray Vining, *Windows for the Crown Prince*	27
1954	James Michener, *Sayonara*	21
1954	Robert Theobald, *The Final Secret of Pearl Harbor*	8
1954	Charles Willoughby and John Chamberlain, *MacArthur, 1941–1951*	7
1955	Michihiko Hachiya, *Hiroshima Diary*	9
1956	Courtney Whitney, *MacArthur: His Rendezvous with History*	6
1957	John Marquand, *Stopover Tokyo*	13
1957	Walter Lord, *Day of Infamy*	17
1957	Gwen Terasaki, *Bridge to the Sun*	4
1958	Alice Ekert-Rotholz, *The Time of the Dragons*	16
1958-59	"Pappy" Boyington, *Baa Baa Black Sheep*	37
1960	Elizabeth Gray Vining, *Return to Japan*	4
1961	Oliver Statler, *Japanese Inn*	23
1962	John Toland, *But Not in Shame*	4
1964-65	Ian Fleming, *You Only Live Twice*	23
1964-65	Douglas MacArthur, *Reminiscences*	30
1967-68	Walter Lord, *Incredible Victory*	21

Source: Author survey of *New York Times* best-seller lists, 1941-1973.

the "Madame Butterfly theme" (see Chapter 5) arises during the occupation, although its origins can be traced back to the original story of Madame Butterfly as well as to Lafcadio Hearn, and the great American infatuation with traditional Japanese culture began with the tourist boom of the late 1950s and early 1960s, although it too has antecedents in

Lafcadio Hearn and Ernest Fenollosa. But themes, regardless of when they emerge, have a tendency to persist. The theme of Hiroshima, for example, runs through the late 1940s, '50s, and '60s like a recurring refrain.

In pursuing the themes that I believe have shaped American thinking about Japan during the last thirty-five years, I have not stuck exclusively to the best-seller list. I have also looked at a great variety of articles in popular magazines. Many of the best-selling books also appeared in magazines, to reach an even wider audience. For example, John Hersey's *Hiroshima* first appeared in the *New Yorker,* and both Elizabeth Gray Vining's *Windows for the Crown Prince* and Gwen Terasaki's *Bridge to the Sun* were excerpted in the *Reader's Digest;* John Marquand's *Stopover Tokyo* appeared in the *Saturday Evening Post* and James Michener's *Sayonara* appeared in *McCall's.* Michihiko Hachiya's *Hiroshima Diary* was excerpted in *Look,* while Courtney Whitney's *MacArthur: His Rendezvous with History* was featured in *Life;* MacArthur's own *Reminiscences* ran in seven issues of *Life* and two of *Reader's Digest.*

But magazines also reveal certain trends in American thought not covered by the best sellers. The most recent best seller dealing with Japan appeared in 1967–68.[17] Since then, however, there has been a steady stream of articles in magazines such as *Time, Newsweek, Business Week,* and *Fortune* about Japanese industry, economic growth, and exports— not subjects that lend themselves to treatment in popular book form, perhaps, but that have nevertheless received wide coverage and had an impact on American attitudes.

Out of such disparate sources as best sellers, popular magazine articles, movies, art exhibits, tourism, business relations, and exports, I have tried to draw a group of themes that I believe have colored

---

[17] In mid-1975, just as this book was going to press, a new historical novel about Japan—James Clavell's *Shōgun*—reached the best-seller list. If nothing else, this book demonstrates that neither American ambivalence toward Japan nor the stereotyped imagery have disappeared. Clavell's novel is set in the seventeenth century and deals with an English pilot who, after his crippled ship lands in Japan, becomes caught up in the power struggle between two feudal lords. In the process, the English pilot is both shocked and attracted by the culture. His Japanese captors teach him, among other things, about karma and patience: "Patience means holding back your inclination to the seven emotions: hate, adoration, joy, anxiety, anger, grief, fear." And from his Japanese mistress he learns that the Japanese "have no word for 'love' as I understand you to mean it. Duty, loyalty, honor, respect, desire, those words and thoughts are what we have, all that we need." Ah, so.

American postwar attitudes toward Japan. Of course, I do not think that all of these themes are equally salient at any given time, or that every American is equally susceptible to every theme. But, generally speaking, the next six chapters summarize what can be gleaned from the floating world of popular stereotypes. A final chapter spells out some of the implications that such American stereotypes about Japan may have for the future relations between our two countries.

2
The Legacy of the War

When one rereads the news stories, books, and novels that came out of the Pacific war, it is not difficult to see why it has had such a strong hold on the American imagination. It began in a highly dramatic, shocking way with a surprise attack that cost 2,500 American lives, compared to only fifty-five Japanese lives. This was followed by a series of painful defeats—MacArthur's retreat from Bataan, the fall of Corregidor, the loss of Wake Island—and some almost equally costly "successes"—the naval battles of the Coral Sea and Midway, and the seesaw battle for Guadalcanal. It was a war against an enemy whom Americans at first underestimated—the "Japs" were thought to be scrawny, near-sighted, and poorly trained and equipped—and whom they soon came to regard as not quite human, endowed with a strange mixture of animal cunning and ability to live in the jungle, and a superhuman devotion to their emperor that went as far as a readiness to die in battle or commit suicide for him.

It is, of course, natural in the midst of a war to paint the enemy in shades of black and to cheer his losses and mourn one's own. But there was a quality to Americans' feelings about the Japanese that was quite different from their reactions to the Germans. During the early years of the war, the Office of War Information analyzed American films to see how Hollywood was portraying the enemy, as well as what sort of messages about our own goals were being conveyed. According to a recent study based on these OWI analyses,

> Hollywood had a distinct view of each of the enemies. Germans were gentlemen with whom it was possible to deal as equals. As soldiers they were efficient, disciplined, and patriotic; the bureau was unable to find a scene in which the

17

Germans were morally corrupt or delighted in cruelty. . . . Japanese soldiers were pictured as less military than their German counterparts, and were almost universally cruel and ruthless. Japanese were short, thin, and wore spectacles. They were tough but devoid of scruples. In almost every film showing American-Japanese battles, the enemy broke the rules of civilized warfare.[1]

One reason, I think, for such portrayals of the Japanese was American unfamiliarity with and distaste for jungle warfare. This comes through in many of the firsthand accounts of ground fighting in the Pacific, but it is most palpable in Norman Mailer's best-selling war novel, *The Naked and the Dead*. The abiding atmosphere of that book is one of sheer physical misery—the oppressive climate, the brutal terrain, the cruel exertions demanded of the soldiers.

> In the first week of the campaign the jungle was easily the General's worst opponent. The division task force had been warned that the forests of Anopopei were formidable, but being told this did not make it easier. Through the densest portions, a man would lose an hour in moving a few hundred feet. In the heart of the forests great trees grew almost a hundred yards high, their lowest limbs sprouting out two hundred feet from the ground. Beneath them, filling the space, grew other trees whose shrubbery hid the giant ones from view. And in the little room left, a choked assortment of vines and ferns, wild banana trees, stunted palms, flowers, brush and shrubs squeezed against each other, raised their burdened leaves to the doubtful light that filtered through, sucking for air and food like snakes at the bottom of a pit. In the deep jungle it was always as dark as the sky before a summer thunderstorm, and no air ever stirred. Everything was damp and rife and hot as though the jungle were an immense collection of oily rags growing hotter and hotter under the dark stifling vaults of a huge warehouse. Heat licked at everything, and the foliage, responding, grew to prodigious sizes. In the depths, in the heat and moisture, it was never silent. The birds cawed, the small animals and occasional snakes rustled and squealed, and beneath it all was a hush, almost palpable, in which could be heard the rapt absorbed sounds of vegetation growing.[2]

---

[1] Gregory D. Black and Clayton R. Koppes, "OWI Goes to the Movies," *Foreign Service Journal*, August 1974, pp. 18-23, 29-30. Also in *Prologue: The Journal of the National Archives*, 6 (1974), pp. 44-59.

[2] Norman Mailer, *The Naked and the Dead* (New York: New American Library, c. 1948), p. 37.

Beside these difficulties, the Japanese seemed almost incidental, as Mailer is often at pains to point out: "The men had not thought about the Japanese at all while they were in the jungle; the denseness of the brush, the cruelty of the river, had absorbed all their attention. The last thing they had considered was an ambush. . . . Once more they forgot about the Japanese, forgot about the patrol, almost forgot about themselves. The only ecstasy they could imagine would be to stop climbing."[3]

And yet the Japanese operated in this territory, and therefore so must the Americans. At times the Japanese seemed to be almost at home in it. John Hersey writes:

> In news accounts of the fighting on Bataan I had read about the ingenious ways in which Jap snipers hid themselves in the trees: dressed all in green, hands and faces painted green, foliage caught in headnets and slung from the waist—all made to look exactly like parts of the trees into which they were tied once and for all. . . . Now I comprehended for the first time why the marines had been taking so few prisoners. It was not just that the boys were trigger-happy, as one had boasted. It was not just brutality, not just vindictive remembrance of Pearl Harbor. Here in the jungle a marine killed because he must, or be killed. He stalked the enemy, and the enemy stalked him, as if each were a hunter tracking a bear cat.

And a marine tells Hersey,

> They're full of tricks. . . . You'll see that when you go into the jungle after them. They hide up in the trees like wildcats. Sometimes when they attack, they scream like a bunch of terrified cattle in a slaughter house. Other times they come on so quiet they wouldn't scare a snake. One of their favorite tricks is to fire their machine guns off to one side. That starts you shooting. Then they start their main fire under the noise of your own shooting. Sometimes they use fire-crackers as a diversion. Other times they jabber to cover the noise of their men cutting through the underbrush with machetes. You've probably heard about their using white surrender flags to suck us into traps. We're onto that one now.[4]

Americans learned to fight in the jungle, but this was never their preferred style of battle—just as years later they had difficulty in adjusting to guerrilla warfare in Vietnam. In Mailer's novel, the Americans

---

[3] Ibid., pp. 385, 544.

[4] John Hersey, *Into the Valley* (New York: Alfred A. Knopf, 1944), pp. 55, 20-21.

merely muddle through. Despite massive miscalculations on the part of the leadership, petty treacheries by lesser figures, and the total failure of the patrol whose efforts constitute the heart of the novel, the American campaign is won by a fluke. Once defeated, however, the Japanese, too, are cut down to size: "It was discovered from questioning the few prisoners that for over a month the Japanese had been on half rations, and toward the end there had been almost no food at all. A Japanese supply dump had been destroyed by artillery five weeks before, and no one had known it. Their medical facilities had been exhausted. . . . Finally they discovered that the Japanese ammunition had been almost depleted a week before the last attack had begun." [5] During the mopping up operations, thousands of Japanese are killed, and Mailer describes several incidents throughout the novel in which Japanese prisoners are shot out of hand. Yet his tone is one not of moral indignation but of profound pessimism: the war is pointless, he seems to say. In America and Europe it will strengthen right-wing, fascist elements (this is one of the political arguments of the book), and Japan will not change. His most searching comment about Japan is put into the mouth of a Japanese-American translator for the American troops. Wakara (it is his only appearance in the book) was in Japan until he was twelve and remembers the physical beauty of the country. But

> behind the beauty it was all bare, with nothing in their lives but toil and abnegation. They were abstract people, who had elaborated an abstract art, and thought in abstractions and spoke in them, devised involuted ceremonies for saying nothing at all, and lived in the most intense fear of their superiors that any people had ever had. And a week ago a battalion of those wistful people had charged to their death with great terrifying screams. Oh, he understood, Wakara thought, why the Americans who had been in Japan hated the Japanese worst of all. Before the war they had been so wistful, so charming; the Americans had picked them up like pets, and were feeling the fury now of having a pet bite them. . . . Well, there was nothing he could do about it. The Americans would march in eventually and after twenty or thirty years the country would probably be the same again, and the people would live in their artistic abstract rut, and begin generating some more juice for another hysterical immolation.[6]

[5] Mailer, *The Naked and the Dead,* p. 554.
[6] Ibid., p. 196.

Next to their adeptness at jungle warfare, it was this quality of self-immolation—their apparent readiness to die—that made Japanese seem either sub- or super-human to Americans. Richard Tregaskis quotes Colonel Edson on the Tulagi campaign:

> The Japanese casualties were about 400. Not a single Nip gave up. (One prisoner was taken; he had been dazed by a close mortar burst.) In one of the holes there were seventeen dead Japs, when a man went in to get the radio. But there were still two Nips alive. They hit the man and one other who followed him later. . . . The snipers would lie still until our men passed, then shoot from the rear. . . . In one case there were three Japs cornered. They had one pistol. They fired the pistol until they had three shots left. Then one Jap shot the two others and killed himself.[7]

At the same time, there were plenty of examples during this and other wars of Americans who single-handedly stormed machine-gun nests, who piloted their crippled airplanes directly into targets, or who bravely went down with the ship. *Time* magazine reported that when the *Yorktown* was going down "two carpenter's mates and a petty officer were trapped in a compartment five decks below. The telephones were still working. Somebody called down: 'Do you know what kinda fix you're in?' 'Sure,' they called back, 'We know you can't get us out, but we got a helluva good acey-deucey game goin' down here right now.' "[8] Richard Tregaskis tells of a private who, "knowing he was hit badly, had asked one of his buddies to give him a .45 automatic, and said: 'You guys better move out. I'm done for anyhow. With that automatic, I can get three or four of the bastards before I kick off.' "[9] But somehow when such stories were told about our own men they aroused pride and amazement at the men's bravery, whereas when similar accounts were told about the other side, people shook their heads at the men's misguided foolhardiness or fanaticism. It was not until twenty-two years after the end of the war that Walter Lord could write as movingly about the sinking of the *Hiryu* at Midway (Admiral Yamaguchi and Captain Kaku went down with the ship, and as the Rising Sun flag was lowered bugles played the national anthem, *Kimigayo*) as he did about

---

[7] Richard Tregaskis, *Guadalcanal Diary* (New York: Random House, 1943), pp. 80, 81, 83.

[8] *Time* magazine, 28 September 1942, p. 37.

[9] Tregaskis, *Guadalcanal Diary*, p. 239.

the sinking of the *Yorktown*. And even then, Lord seems to play for laughs the scene in which Ensign Sandanori Kawakami, the young paymaster on the *Hiryu* who was also custodian of the Emperor's portrait, made the momentous decision to pack the portrait in his rucksack and transfer it to another ship.

Postwar Accounts of the Pacific War

It is instructive, in looking at American attitudes toward the Pacific war, to compare Walter Lord's two books with each other and with the wartime accounts that preceded them. Lord's narrative technique is very similar to that of reporters such as John Hersey and Richard Tregaskis. Like them, he concentrates on "the little people" in a battle—the privates, sergeants, cooks, and medics. In *Men on Bataan,* John Hersey uses this technique in an almost cloying way. After describing a particularly brave or harrowing American encounter with the enemy, he writes: "I think you ought to meet the private who, when the flames spread, climbed right up on the pile of smoldering, exploding ammunition. He was Harry J. Slagle, from Lancaster, South Carolina." [10] (This litany—"I think you ought to meet"—recurs throughout the book.) Richard Tregaskis, in *Guadalcanal Diary,* simply identifies all his sources in parentheses: "A few minutes later I caught up with the temporary command post in a grove of trees. Major (now Lieutenant Colonel) Bill Phipps (William I. Phipps of Omaha, Nebraska) was riding a captured Jap bicycle up and down a track road which cut through the woods." [11] Obviously, one of the attractions of these books at the time they were first published was to read about the exploits of men whom you might have known back home.

Walter Lord retains the technique of naming as many individual participants as possible, and he tells his story in the breathless, you-are-there style of the wartime correspondents. However, since Lord constructed his narratives from hundreds of interviews with participants, and with the benefit of other written accounts, he is in a sense like a reporter who can be everywhere and know everything at once. What he has lost is the immediacy of the reporter and the reporter's own voice and reactions. Since Lord is writing as a historian, this is of course not a failing,

---

[10] John Hersey, *Men on Bataan* (New York: Knopf, 1942), p. 146.
[11] Tregaskis, *Guadalcanal Diary,* pp. 54-55.

provided there is a substitution of historical judgments for the gut reactions that are no longer present. Unfortunately, Lord's narrative style leaves very little room for such historical assessments.

Walter Lord's greater distance from his subject shows in a variety of ways. Whereas Hersey and Tregaskis refer as freely to "Japs" and "Nips" as do the marines they are quoting, Lord always writes about the "Japanese," except when he is quoting someone directly or describing someone's thoughts in the heat of battle. Lord also begins to describe events from both sides, although in *Day of Infamy* only 39 pages out of 218 are devoted to the Japanese end of things. A truly bifocal account of Pearl Harbor was only attempted with the film *Tora! Tora! Tora!* in 1970. *Incredible Victory* is more even-handed: 105 out of 297 pages deal with the Japanese side of the battle of Midway, and an effort is made to convey the emotions and fears of the Japanese as well as their strategic thinking. It is worth speculating why *Incredible Victory* should be so much more even-handed than *Day of Infamy*. Are Americans more likely to give the other side its just dues when the outcome of the battle is a victory for our side? Or does Pearl Harbor continue to rankle so despite the passage of time that we can only see it as a dastardly act? Or, again, is it that *Day of Infamy* was published in 1957, whereas *Incredible Victory* appeared ten years later—the intervening years having served to soften American memories of the war and also having made it considerably easier for an American historian to do the necessary research and interviewing in Japan? I personally tend to favor the latter interpretation. Time has erased much of the bitterness surrounding the World War II battles between the United States and Japan, so that the continuing fascination with books about these battles is probably due to the fact that they are merely "good yarns."

One also sees this lessening of animosity toward the Japanese in a belated personal account by someone who might well consider himself entitled to hold a grudge: "Pappy" Boyington, an ace fighter pilot who was a prisoner-of-war of the Japanese for eighteen months. Boyington's *Baa Baa Black Sheep* was a surprise best seller from mid-1958 until well into 1959—a surprise to literary commentators who found the book to be a boozy, ungrammatical account of the adventures of a marine ace full of trite philosophy, and evidently a surprise to Boyington as well, because friends had told him that he was too late with a war book. "I hear it said again and again to me (and I am getting a little weary of the same old disc): 'But, Boyington, the whole trouble with you is you're so late.' " [12]

Actually, given the fact that Boyington was rather pro-Japanese and anti-Chinese, he probably published his book at precisely the right time. (He also illustrates once again that Americans are not likely to be simultaneously fond of both of these Asian nations.) Nineteen fifty-eight was, of course, a good year to be anti-Chinese, but Boyington's animosities go back to some early 1941 flying that he did under Claire Chennault with the American Volunteer Group, which later became the Flying Tigers. One reason why Boyington got out when the group achieved that more formal status is that he wanted to remain in the Marine Corps instead of joining the Air Force. While in China, Boyington also developed a strong dislike for the Chinese and their leaders:

> The informer method, which I found so prevalent out in China, one person getting ahead of another by turning his compatriots in for gold or favor, made me become more and more anti-social as the years went by. . . . Something else became clear. The yellow-skinned bums weren't with the United States against the Japanese. They were all fighting for power within China, standing by for an opportunity to take over. . . . Personally I couldn't see how Chennault figured them. It was so obvious that the Generalissimo was nothing but a front who never said anything on his own or even thought for himself. The Madame did everything. Chiang Kai-shek just seemed to be led around where she wanted him to be led, and, right or wrong, I was positive that the Madame was a number-one con artist if I had ever seen one.[13]

Boyington's more favorable impression of the Japanese stems in part from the fact that as a fighter pilot he dealt with Japanese Zero and bomber pilots on a one-to-one basis; like gladiators, the two groups of fliers had a good deal of respect for each other. After he was shot down and captured, Boyington was often treated badly—he was beaten, questioned at great length, fed poorly, and his wounds were deliberately left untreated—but he always distinguished between "good Japs" and "bad Japs." While he was still on Saipan (before he was transferred to Japan) a Japanese warrant officer came up to him and asked the interpreter who was with him to translate. The interpreter said, " 'I'm not able to trans-

---

[12] "Pappy" [Colonel Gregory] Boyington, *Baa Baa Black Sheep* (New York: G. P. Putnam's Sons, 958), p. 276.

[13] Ibid., pp. 90, 92, 105.

late the exact words, but I will give you the message as best I can. He says he would like to have you know the majority of the Japanese are ashamed of the way you are being treated, but to have faith, because the horrible war shall be over before too long. Then we shall all be friends again.' " [14] Boyington also learned to distinguish between the gung-ho and often brutal military types and some of the more intellectual Japanese whom he met, chiefly as translators. "There was many a college professor, as well as American-educated Japanese, who had been inducted into the movement of Asia for the Asians, with the industrialized nation of Japan on top, of course. Many of this type individual were employed with a reserve military status as interpreters. I believed the majority of them when they said they didn't have a thing to say about the matter. And were in a boat similar to ours [the prisoners']. The Japs didn't trust them, either." [15] He was angry that many of these people were so poorly treated during the occupation's purges, even when he and other prisoners wrote depositions on their behalf.

Toward the end of the war, Boyington and other prisoners worked outside the prison helping to clear away the rubble caused by American bombing. Of this experience he writes: "I really got to know the population of Japan quite well. In our daily work of removing the destroyed homes of the Japanese civilians, and even when they had lost members of their families, relatives, or friends, I did not seem to notice any belligerence toward us. I walked by the crowds of civilians, within three or four feet of them, in rags and half starved, and never once did I have any occasion to fear them, before or after the B-29 raids." [16]

A similar picture of wartime Japan was painted by Gwen Terasaki in *Bridge to the Sun* (1957). Mrs. Terasaki was the American-born wife of a Japanese diplomat, and in 1942 she and her husband and child returned to Japan for the duration of the war and the early years of the occupation. She, too, gave Americans one of their first sympathetic pictures of how the average Japanese civilian felt during the war, and of the hardships he endured. As the wife of a liberal and cosmopolitan Japanese (who was in retirement during the war because he was distrusted by the military clique that ran the government), she also tried to convey something of the anguish felt by many highly placed Japanese who did not want, and tried to prevent, a war with the United States.

[14] Ibid., p. 269.
[15] Ibid., p. 307.
[16] Ibid., p. 333.

Attitudes toward the Emperor

One of the earliest wartime attempts to present such a differentiated portrait of the Japanese to the American people took the form of a record of another, often happier era. In 1944, the former ambassador to Japan, Joseph Grew, published his diary for the years 1932–42, and it was on the best-seller list from 4 June until 29 October. Grew undoubtedly had a purpose in mind in publishing this book when he did. He had returned to the United States in August 1942 (in the same exchange of diplomats and nationals that took Terasaki to Japan), and he had lectured widely throughout the United States on the dangers of underestimating the Japanese war-making machine. At the same time, he had lived in Japan too long and he had worked too hard with Japanese liberals in trying to prevent the war to view all Japanese as fanatical madmen. Aside from the details of the negotiations and maneuverings that preceded Pearl Harbor, what shines through the pages of Grew's diary is a picture of a nation which contained many capable, sensible, and civilized people as well as a clique of militarists bent on war. This was precisely what Grew wanted to convey:

> In the heat and prejudice of war some will deny that there can be any good elements among the Japanese people. Yet those critics, in all likelihood, will not have known personally and directly those Japanese who were bitterly opposed to war with the United States—men who courageously but futilely gave all that was in them and ran the gravest dangers of imprisonment if not of assassination—indeed several were assassinated—in their efforts to stem the tide or, let us say, to halt the tidal wave of insane military megalomania and expansionist ambition. Those people must and will loyally support their leaders in war; those who have to fight must and will fight to the end. But we shall need to know and to weigh all factors in approaching the difficult postwar problems. It is my hope that these intimate, day-to-day records may serve to produce for the future a wider and more helpful picture of those people as people.[17]

Well before the war with Japan had ended, while Grew was first a special assistant to the secretary of state and then director of the Office of Far Eastern Affairs in the State Department, a debate had begun within

---

[17] Joseph C. Grew, *Ten Years in Japan* (New York: Simon and Schuster, 1944), p. xi.

the American government about how Japan should be treated in defeat. Grew and others who knew Japan well favored the complete destruction of her military might and the forced liberalization of her society, but they did not favor wiping out the entire upper class in Japan—a sort of imposed French Revolution. Those who did favor such a drastic course of action included some who felt extremely bitter toward the Japanese—the *New York Times* journalist Otto Tolischus, for example, who had been imprisoned by the Japanese from the time of Pearl Harbor until he was repatriated along with Grew and others—and some who for ideological reasons wanted to see Japan rebuilt along leftist, socialist lines. In this latter group one might include the scholar T. A. Bisson (who was in China during the late 1920s and may be another example of an American whose affection for the Chinese colored his opinions of the Japanese) and the journalist I. F. Stone. Leftist hopes for Japan ultimately blossomed into a vocal school of criticism of the occupation (discussed in Chapter 4), but in the days preceding and immediately following the end of the war, the argument centered on the person and institution of the Japanese emperor.

Grew (and knowledgeable anthropologists such as Ruth Benedict) favored the retention of the emperor as the symbolic head of the nation. Others, such as Otto Tolischus, argued that the emperor system "is the greatest obstacle to Japanese democracy and the bulwark from behind which the Japanese militarists, industrialists and bureaucrats control the land. Above all, it is the source of Japanese fanaticism and the inspiration for Japan's career of conquest. . . . The simplest way of ending it would be to do away with the Emperor entirely and to see to it that no member of the present dynasty ever ascends the throne." Tolischus, however, concentrated on the wartime ideals propagated in the name of the emperor, ideals which Tolischus argued were "based on an irrational religious fanaticism coupled with savagery. . . . Shinto is a faith without theology or doctrine, without ethics or morals, without a clear distinction between good or evil." [18] T. A. Bisson had something else in mind when he wrote, "Maintenance of the Emperor will keep the old ruling groups in power and seriously prejudice any possibility of reorganizing Japanese society on a democratic basis." Shortly after the surrender, he further defined this reorganization as "a swift overturn through popular revolt, on every count the safest form of political insurance with respect to

---

[18] Otto Tolischus, "God-emperor: Key to a Nation," *New York Times Magazine,* 19 August 1945, pp. 8, 33.

27

postwar Japan. . . . The quintessence of a correct [American] policy toward Japan is to help the people throw out the oligarchy." [19] I. F. Stone attacked Grew as a representative of the wealthy Groton-Harvard aristocracy whose "contacts were with the upper classes in Japan as those of his British counterpart, Sir Nevile Henderson, were with the upper classes in Germany." [20] Others associated the former ambassador with "British and American tories who declare that the Emperor must be kept in a beaten Japan as a safeguard against Communism." [21]

The average American had no strong opinions one way or the other in this sectarian argument. During the war, Americans had developed a curiosity about Mikadoism—this strange belief that enabled Japanese to fight so fiercely and die so freely. But once the war was over, there was no widespread residual hatred toward the emperor, as there was toward Tojo, Yamashita, and other well-known military figures. On 11 August 1945, when the *New York Times* banner headline read "JAPAN OFFERS TO SURRENDER: U.S. MAY LET EMPEROR REMAIN; MASTER RECONVERSION PLAN SET" (with a smaller headline underneath reading "Truman Is Said to Favor Retention of Hirohito as Spiritual Leader"), there was a smaller story datelined Guam on the lower front page which was headed: "GI's in Pacific Go Wild With Joy; 'Let 'Em Keep Emperor,' They Say." And on an inside page, an analytical article about Hirohito and the nature of Shintoism ended by saying "The Emperor is regarded not so much as an active ruler but rather as the source of authority. His advisers exercise this authority and they, not the Emperor, in Japanese eyes are responsible for mistakes. He is, essentially, the passive keystone of the political and social structure of Japan." [22]

The ultimate fate of the emperor was settled by Douglas MacArthur (the "clarification" the Japanese had received prior to agreeing to surrender was not that the emperor's sovereignty would necessarily remain inviolate but merely that it would be subject to the Supreme Commander of the Allied Powers, SCAP). According to Courtney Whitney,

---

[19] T. A. Bisson, "The Japanese Discuss Their 'Sacred Mission,' " [review of Otto Tolischus, *Through Japanese Eyes*] *The New York Times Book Review,* 15 April 1945, p. 6; and "Japan's Strategy of Revival," *New Republic,* 27 August 1945, pp. 242-43.

[20] Quoted in Andrew Roth, *Dilemma in Japan* (Boston: Little, Brown and Company, 1945), p. 36.

[21] Ibid., p. 35.

[22] *New York Times,* 11 August 1945, p. 4.

MacArthur was under some pressure from the British and the Russians to put Hirohito on trial as a war criminal. "MacArthur stoutly resisted such efforts. Finally, when Washington seemed to be veering toward the British point of view, he advised that he would need at least one million reinforcements should such action be taken. He believed that if the Emperor were indicted as a war criminal, military government would have to be instituted throughout all Japan, and guerrilla warfare might break out. The Emperor's name was stricken off the list." [23] Subsequent steps to limit the power of the emperor—his specific disavowal of divine status, the constitutional stipulation that he could exercise no political power, and the abolition of the crime of lèse-majesté—were all carried out at MacArthur's behest.

What American doubts may have remained about the essential benignity of the Japanese emperor were laid to rest not by these actions, however, but by the publication of an unusual best seller: Elizabeth Gray Vining's *Windows for the Crown Prince*. Chock-full of Japanese names which could not possibly have much meaning to an American audience—Katsunoshin Yamanashi, Prince Higashikuni, Grand Chamberlains Shiro Sumikura and Shigeto Hozumi, Grand Steward Yoshitami Matsudaira—this book would probably not draw flies today. But in 1952 it was on the best-seller list for twenty-seven weeks, attesting to the curiosity Americans still had about the Japanese emperor and his family.

In the spring of 1946, the emperor had mentioned to an American delegation of educators that he would like an American tutor for his eldest son, Crown Prince Akihito, specifying only that the tutor should be a woman, "a Christian, but not a fanatic," and not an "old Japan hand." After an informal selection process the choice finally settled on Elizabeth Gray Vining, then a 44-year-old widow who had written a number of books for children and who was a devout Quaker. She arrived in Japan in the fall of 1946 and gave English lessons not only to the crown prince but also to several other of the "imperial children" and to the empress herself until the end of 1950. Her book, *Windows for the Crown Prince*, makes strange reading for an American today because it strikes one as both fatuous and presumptuous: Vining involving her entire Japanese household in morning Bible readings, Vining teaching

---

[23] Courtney Whitney, *MacArthur: His Rendezvous with History* (New York: Knopf, 1956), p. 284. Interestingly enough, MacArthur's own description is almost word-for-word the same. See Douglas MacArthur, *Reminiscences* (New York: McGraw-Hill, 1964), p. 288.

her young charges about William Penn and the Indians so that they would learn about peaceful relationships between people of differing races and countries, about the Olympic Games because of their expressed purpose of "not victory but partnership," and about Pierre Ceresole, "whose Service Civile Internationale offered the moral equivalent of war that William James advocated." [24] Yet she so obviously meant well, had great tact and respect for Japanese culture, and was far less presumptuous in her goals and methods than many members of the occupation. The great appeal of her book to Americans was the intimate glimpses she provided of the imperial family. She seems to have satisfied her audience so thoroughly on this score that her 1960 sequel, *Return to Japan*—an account of the wedding of the Crown Prince to a "commoner"—was on the best-seller list only briefly.

For Americans in general, the Japanese emperor ceased to be an enigma—and therefore ceased to be interesting—with the publication of Vining's book. But the hostility that motivated Tolischus, Bisson, Stone, and others is still capable of rousing some people to fever pitch. In 1971, a book of truly manic proportions (1,239 pages) was published by David Bergamini, arguing that Emperor Hirohito was not a passive figurehead during the war but its archvillain. *Japan's Imperial Conspiracy* was roundly panned by most knowledgeable reviewers—James Crowley called it "completely unsubstantiated by any reliable source, primary or secondary" [25]—although Bergamini would doubtless maintain that these attacks were launched by establishment scholars who were in league with the Japanese power-structure. Bergamini's own motives in writing the book are by no means clear, however. He was born in Japan, the son of an architect who in 1936 moved to China. In 1939, the family made its way to the Philippines where they were eventually interned by the Japanese for the duration of the war. Life was hard in the internment camp, and Bergamini may be trying to settle some complex personal score with the Japanese. However, he is also a professional writer (though not in any sense a scholar of Japanese history or politics) and he may merely have been searching for something new and sensational to say about the war with Japan. Whatever the case, and whatever the merits of his argument, it is clear that he went on at almost interminable length and that the American public simply was not interested. His book

---

[24] Elizabeth Gray Vining, *Windows for the Crown Prince* (New York: J. B. Lippincott, 1952), pp. 157, 208.

[25] *New York Times Book Review,* 24 October 1971, p. 3.

not only never made the best-seller list, it was being remaindered a bare two years after it was published.

In some respects Bergamini's belated obsession and its reception are an index of American attitudes toward the war in the Pacific. The savagery and unanticipated hardships of that war produced great hostility toward the "Japs." No doubt for some individuals this hostility has never waned. But the majority of Americans, while still capable of getting excited by a rousing account of Pearl Harbor or the battle of Midway, are no longer very interested in castigating their former enemy. As for the emperor who once inspired the Japanese to such efforts, Elizabeth Gray Vining's picture of him as the gentle marine biologist of Sagami Bay seems to have stuck. My guess is that it would take nothing less than another war to change that image.

3
The Legacy of Hiroshima

The attitudes of Americans toward the events of 6 August 1945 are a good deal more complex than their attitudes toward those of 7 December 1941. One reason, perhaps, is that Americans were the actors in 1945—they dropped an atomic bomb on Hiroshima—whereas on Pearl Harbor Day they were acted upon. It is always easier to attach an unambiguous label to someone else's behavior than to one's own. President Roosevelt's characterization of 7 December 1941 as "a date which will live in infamy" may have faded somewhat, but it has certainly not disappeared from the national vocabulary, whereas attitudes toward Hiroshima have become hedged about with self-justification, feelings of guilt, and doubt. Was it necessary to drop the bomb? Could the war have been won without it? Should we have issued a warning or held a demonstration first? Was it a racist act, something we would not have done in the war with Germany? Was the dropping of an A-bomb morally justifiable under any circumstances? Such questions have undoubtedly helped to soften our attitudes toward the Japanese in the postwar period: if they were beastly during the war, we were beastly too. But, paradoxically, our guilt feelings may also cause us to dislike the Japanese more. We not only tend to avoid people who make us feel guilty, we also tend to "project" our own feelings of guilt, so that the victim becomes transformed into an accuser whom we can then hate for accusing us. It is a well-known psychological mechanism in unhappy marriages, and it can equally well color relationships between nations and peoples.

It is important to recall, however, that, just as unhappy marriages may once have been happy, the news of Hiroshima was not initially surrounded by an aura of American guilt. One senses in the news reports

33

a feeling of awe—a definite awareness that we had entered the atomic age—but this is coupled with a steely determination to end the war. In his announcement concerning the bomb, President Truman said: "It was to spare the Japanese people from utter destruction that the ultimatum of July 26 was issued at Potsdam. Their leaders promptly rejected that ultimatum. If they do not now accept our terms, they may expect a rain of ruin from the air the like of which has never been seen on this earth." [1] The following day the *New York Times* reported Curtis LeMay as saying that if the same weapon had been available to the American Air Force as late as February 1943, there would have been no need for the invasion of Europe. The general feeling was that should Japan itself be invaded the Japanese were prepared to fight down to the last man, woman, and child (there had been broadcasts in Japan urging them to do precisely that), and the atomic bomb was intended to shock, or scare, them into surrender. Lieutenant General Leslie R. Groves, head of the Manhattan Project that built the bomb, has argued that his goal was "to bring the war to an end sooner than it would otherwise be ended, and thus to save American lives. We were losing about 250 men a day in the Pacific. The estimated American casualties for landing on Japanese shores were anywhere between 250,000 and 1,000,000 while the Japanese casualties were conservatively estimated to run as high as 10 million." [2] Colonel Paul W. Tibbets, the pilot of the "Enola Gay" (a B-29 named after his mother) which dropped the bomb on Hiroshima, later said, "I thought it would take five atom bombs to jar the Japanese into quitting." [3]

After a second atomic bomb had been dropped on Nagasaki on 9 August, the *New York Times* reported that "the Japanese knew now that our atomic bombing of Hiroshima, in which 60 percent of the urban area was wiped out, was no one-shot performance"; and Truman warned, "We shall continue to use it [the atomic bomb] until we completely destroy Japan's power to make war. Only a Japanese surrender will stop us." [4] The next day the headline said: "JAPAN OFFERS TO SURRENDER."

---

[1] *New York Times,* 7 August 1945, p. 1.

[2] *New York Times Magazine,* 1 August 1965, p. 9.

[3] Paul W. Tibbets, Jr., as told to Wesley Price, "How to Drop an A-Bomb," *Saturday Evening Post,* 8 June 1946, p. 18.

[4] *New York Times,* 10 August 1945, p. 1.

The Initial Reaction

In the months immediately following the surrender, several factual
accounts appeared in newspapers and in magazines such as *Life* analyzing the damage inflicted on Hiroshima and Nagasaki. As early as
20 August 1945, *Life* reported a figure of 100,000 dead in Hiroshima,
belying later charges that Americans have always tended to minimize
the number killed there (63,000-78,000 is usually given as the "American" figure, whereas some Japanese estimates range as high as 240,000).[5]
But Americans were more curious about the bomb's secret development
and how it had been dropped than about its effect on Japan. In the
8 June 1946 issue of the *Saturday Evening Post,* Colonel Tibbets
described in detail how the 509th Composite Group, which he had
commanded, was trained to drop an atomic bomb without being told
precisely what it was they were being trained to drop. Bombardier
accuracy was a great requirement of the mission because "the atom
bomb should convince the Japanese that surrender time was now. It
wouldn't be overwhelmingly convincing if we fumbled the bomb into an
empty rice paddy. To unsell the Japanese on war, the atom bombs had
to hit big industrial targets dead center." Tibbets was unreservedly proud
of his own crew's accuracy over Hiroshima, and whenever asked "How
do you feel about the mission?" he said he was tempted to answer with
the question " 'How do you feel?' We're all living in the Atomic Age
together, and the atom bomb was made and dropped for the people
of the United States."

MGM made two movies about the development and dropping of
the A-bomb. The first, called *The Beginning of the End,* was released
on 20 February 1947, and featured such stars as Brian Donlevy as
General Leslie Groves, Hume Cronyn as J. Robert Oppenheimer, and
Barry Nelson as Colonel Tibbets. Bosley Crowther, the *New York Times*
movie critic, panned the film because it had created two wholly spurious
"love-interest" subplots and because it did not "evince any more than a
miniature span of the full and conglomerate immensity of the subject of
atomic power," but basically he did not disagree with the approach of
the producers of the film, that the development of the atomic bomb

---

5 Twenty-nine years later the official Japanese figure of confirmed deaths—including
those who died in subsequent years of A-bomb related causes—was 84,446 (*Japan
Times,* 24 July 1974).

ranks "as one of the greatest 'thrillers' in the annals of man." The second film, entitled *Above and Beyond,* appeared in January 1953 and featured Robert Taylor as Colonel Tibbets and Eleanor Parker as his wife. It dealt with the training of the 509th Composite Group in Utah and with the strains that secrecy imposed on the Tibbets's marriage. (Colonel Tibbets was the only one who knew of the group's future mission, but of course he could not tell anyone, not even his wife.) Crowther found this film "tediously long and earnest . . . with the greatest emotional stimulation in the account of the Hiroshima trip" with which it ends.

The first eye-witness account of the attack on Hiroshima was published in the *Saturday Review of Literature* on 11 May 1946 by J. A. Siemes, a German Jesuit priest. On 6 August 1945, Siemes was at the Novitiate of the Society of Jesus at Nagatsuka, a small suburban town about two kilometers from Hiroshima. He himself was not hurt, but he and his fellow priests received and cared for many bomb survivors at the novitiate, and he also ventured into Hiroshima on that first day to help rescue several fellow priests, including Father Kleinsorge, who was later interviewed and made famous by John Hersey. Siemes describes the terrible damage done by the bomb, but he is also critical of Japanese rescue efforts: "It became clear to us during these days that the Japanese displayed little initiative, preparedness, and organizational skill in preparation for catastrophe. They failed to carry out any rescue work when something could have been saved by a cooperative effort, and fatalistically let the catastrophe take its course." He also notes that although "the Japanese suffered this terrible blow as part of the fortunes of war" and seemed to harbor no feelings of vengeance toward the Americans, "a few days after the atomic bombing, the secretary of the University came to us asserting that the Japanese were ready to destroy San Francisco by means of an equally effective bomb. It is dubious that he himself believed what he told us. He merely wanted to impress upon us foreigners that the Japanese were capable of similar discoveries. . . . The Japanese also intimated that the principle of the new bomb was a Japanese discovery. It was only lack of raw materials, they said, which prevented its construction." Clearly, this early eye-witness account, although written by a religious man, still treats the Japanese as citizens of a belligerent nation and has not entirely lost the somewhat tough-minded "war-is-war" point of view that even noncombatants adopt during such times.

Hersey's Hiroshima

The account that radically changed American perceptions and feelings about Hiroshima appeared in the 31 August 1946 issue of the *New Yorker*. The author, of course, was John Hersey, then thirty-two years old, who in 1942 had written about "Jap" snipers on Guadalcanal and had approvingly quoted a marine as saying

> I wish we were fighting against Germans. They are human beings, like us. Fighting against them must be like an athletic performance—matching your skill against someone you know is good. Germans are misled, but at least they react like men. But the Japs are like animals. Against them you have to learn a whole new set of physical reactions. You have to get used to their animal stubbornness and tenacity. They take to the jungle as if they had been bred there, and like some beasts you never see them until they are dead.[6]

Hersey's *Hiroshima* is not a personal eye-witness account, but a careful reconstruction of the bomb's dropping and its aftermath as it was experienced by six survivors, five Japanese men and women and one German Jesuit priest, Father Kleinsorge. Hersey used a spare, almost uninflected prose. Charles Poore, the *New York Times* book reviewer, called the result "the quietest, and the best, of all the stories that have been written about the most spectacular explosion in the time of man."

The account made an extraordinary public impact. The *New Yorker* published it *in toto,* devoting an entire issue to the work and banishing from its sidelines all the usual cartoons. The *New York Times* published an editorial on 30 August urging that "every American who has permitted himself to make jokes about atom bombs, or who has come to regard them as just one sensational phenomenon that can now be accepted as part of civilization, like the airplane and the gasoline engine, or who has allowed himself to speculate as to what we might do with them if we were forced into another war, ought to read Mr. Hersey." A number of newspapers reprinted the piece, abiding by Hersey's strictures that the profits be donated to the Red Cross and that the account be published without any cuts. On the evenings of 8–12 September 1946, the American Broadcasting Company cancelled its regular 8:30 to 9 p.m. programming and read Hersey's *Hiroshima* to its audiences, using different actors' and actresses' voices. The Book-of-the-Month Club distrib-

---

[6] See John Hersey, *Into the Valley* (New York: Alfred A. Knopf, 1944), p. 56.

uted a hard-bound edition free of charge to its subscribers, and another hard-bound edition was on the best-seller list for a month. Since 1946, the account has gone through some seven editions and more than fifty printings.

In his *New York Times* review, Charles Poore speculated on the effect Hersey's *Hiroshima* would have on American thought. Letters to the *New Yorker* had run ten to one in favor of the piece; and ABC reported that 95 percent of its letters praised the broadcasts and only 5 percent disapproved, usually on grounds that "the Japs had the bomb coming to them." Poore himself concluded that "nothing that can be said about the book can equal what the book has to say. It speaks for itself, and, in an unforgettable way, for humanity."

It would be more accurate to say that the book does not "speak for itself," and that it is precisely its ambiguous, open quality—the flattened tone, the complete lack of editorial comment by the author—that permitted it to become a best seller in 1946 and that has since made it a classic. Every reader, every generation of readers, can bring a personal interpretation to Hersey's account. In recent times *Hiroshima* has been read as a stark condemnation of the use of the atomic bomb. Yet in 1946, Charles Poore found that among Hersey's readers "there is very little evidence that many believe we should hesitate to use the bomb if anyone ever made aggressive war on us again."

There is no question, however, but that one immediate as well as long-range effect of the book was to elicit American empathy with the Japanese. The very structure of the account was designed to do that; it is easier to identify with six recognizable individuals than to feel for the plight of faceless thousands. Hersey's *Hiroshima* was the first postwar book that restored to Americans their sense of the Japanese as human beings rather than as "the enemy." In the wake of this individuation—the awareness that Japanese had families, jobs, homes, ambitions—there of course came feelings of American guilt; there is an enormous difference between dropping a bomb on an enemy target and dropping a bomb on Miss Toshiko Sasaki, Dr. Masakazu Fujii, and their friends. Much of the same process of individuation was being experienced by the Americans who had been sent to occupy Japan. Again, they were no longer confronting a former enemy, but were now forced to deal with men and women who walked and talked, who had problems, and who were, on occasion, quite beautiful and loveable. Both the occupation and the public impact of Hersey's *Hiroshima* are responsible for the extraordinarily rapid dissipation of wartime stereotypes about Japan. Some of the less fortunate implications of American guilt feelings over Hiroshima surfaced more slowly.

Hersey's book, aside from the fame it brought its author, also brought notoriety to its six real-life characters. Most of them have been interviewed again and again by Americans writing about the bomb. Even Robert Lifton, who is sensitive to the issue of "professional survivors," appears to have interviewed four or five out of Hersey's original six.[7] Lifton also reinterviewed several of the individuals first described by Robert Jungk in his 1961 book, *Children of the Ashes.* Over the years, there has developed a sort of trans-Pacific Hiroshima industry— fueled at various times by American Quakers, pacifists, and leftists, all poking through the same set of ruins. It would be pointless to review here every last product of this industry, primarily because so few had any major national impact comparable to that of Hersey's *Hiroshima.* The leftists wrote for each other in leftist magazines; the religious wrote for each other in *Christian Century* and other publications. Only one other American name is indelibly linked to that of Hiroshima: Norman Cousins.

Cousins's Hiroshima

Cousins has been editor of the *Saturday Review of Literature* continuously (except for a brief spell in 1972–73) since 1940. From 1952 to 1954 he was also president of the United World Federalists; from 1957 to 1963 he was cochairman of the Committee for a Sane Nuclear Policy; and from 1965 to the present he has served as president of the World Association of World Federalists. His personal political views have always permeated the *Saturday Review,* for which he regularly writes the editorials and, sometimes, major articles. His concern over Hiroshima obviously predated the publication of Hersey's book, since the *Saturday Review* was the first magazine in America to publish an eye-witness account of the atomic bomb's damage, but Hersey indirectly set into motion many of Cousins's later activities. One of the Hiroshima survivors described in Hersey's book, Reverend Kiyoshi Tanimoto, took

---

[7] See Robert Lifton, *Death in Life* (New York: Random House, 1967). I say "appears" because Lifton does not identify most of the people he interviewed by name and one must therefore deduce his overlap with authors Hersey, Jungk, and Hachiya from internal evidence—namely, the life-histories themselves.

advantage of his new-found notoriety to make several trips to the United States. In late 1948 and early 1949, Tanimoto was on a speaking tour in the United States designed to raise money for a proposed Peace Center in Hiroshima, which he hoped would include not merely the museum, lecture hall, and cenotaph that were eventually built, but also a library and an entire university devoted to the study of peace. In the 5 March 1949 issue of the *Saturday Review,* Cousins published a short article by Tanimoto outlining his ideas and soliciting funds from readers, and Cousins himself appended a note saying that the project was one that "the editors enthusiastically endorse and with which they will associate themselves." Five months later Cousins was in Hiroshima for the first time, attending the 6 August A-bomb commemorative ceremonies and the ground-breaking of the proposed Peace Center.

For the next twenty years the association between Hiroshima and Norman Cousins was close, and it influenced the attitudes of many Americans. Unlike many pacifists who followed in his wake during the 1950s, Cousins was no weeping, guilt-ridden moralist. From the very first, his attitude was one of Christian cheerfulness. In a speech at the 1949 ground-breaking ceremonies (reprinted in the 3 September 1949 *Saturday Review*) he said, "Four years ago this city was a symbol of destruction. Today it is a symbol of hope. . . . The visitor came to Hiroshima expecting to see the end of the world. He found instead the beginning of a better one." He liked the "frontier atmosphere" of Hiroshima; at the same time, he saw that a great deal needed to be done and that Americans could help. He visited an orphanage, and out of that visit, which he described in another *Saturday Review* article on 17 September 1949, grew the idea that Americans might make "moral adoptions" of such orphans by sending monthly or annual donations toward their maintenance. (It was illegal at the time to adopt Japanese orphans and bring them to the United States.) The flood of responsive letters, only a small sampling of them printed in subsequent issues of the *Saturday Review,* eventually led Cousins to establish a committee to help support Hiroshima orphans.

In the 9 April 1955 issue of the *Saturday Review,* Cousins announced his most ambitious project, the Hiroshima Maidens. Cousins explained that on an earlier trip to Hiroshima (by 1955 he had been there on four previous occasions) Reverend Tanimoto had introduced him to a group of girls badly scarred by radiation burns. Cousins conceived of the idea of bringing them to the United States for plastic surgery. On 14 May 1955 he described for his readers the imminent arrival of twenty-five of these girls in New York, where they would be lodged with various Quaker families and where a team of plastic surgeons would donate their services and Mt. Sinai Hospital make available its facilities free of charge. On 15 October, Cousins furnished readers with an "Interim Report on the Maidens," in which he described how their operations were progressing, and in later reports he also described what various girls were doing—studying art, typing, nursing, cosmetology—as their scars healed. Like Hersey's *Hiroshima,* Cousins's Hiroshima Maidens aroused extraordinary public interest and empathy because, once again, people were able to focus on individuals. Cousins himself seemed to be well aware of the role played by a concern for individuals as opposed to a sense of cosmic guilt in his personal motivation. He was often asked whether his efforts on behalf of the Hiroshima Maidens were to soothe his own conscience, and to this he replied rather abstractly, "Certainly I had guilty feelings—but it was a guilt which extended to war itself, for the real crime concerning the failure of all peoples to bring the causes of war under control. . . . The important thing was to address ourselves to the main business at hand, which was to protect the world's peoples against war itself." [8] But when one of the Hiroshima Maidens died of heart failure shortly after one of her operations, he described a much more personal sense of guilt: "even more insistent was the thought that kept coming back to me—that I had started in motion something that resulted in what was now happening to Tomoko." [9]

It is also worth speculating on the significance of the fact that the burn-victims brought to the United States were all girls. The *New York Times* Asian correspondent Robert Trumbull has argued that, "In the case of women, particularly, these afflictions [the burn scars] have tragic social and economic consequences" [10] but in view of the fact that several of the girls had operations not on their faces but on their hands—to make them usable once again—one wonders whether there were no male Hiroshima victims whose working capacity might have been enhanced by similar operations. It is more likely that girls were chosen (perhaps unconsciously by both the Japanese and Cousins) because they would evoke less hostility and more unalloyed empathy on the part

[8] *Saturday Review of Literature,* 6 August 1955, p. 32.

[9] *Saturday Review of Literature,* 9 June 1956, p. 25.

[10] *New York Times Magazine,* 31 July 1955, p. 21.

of Americans. Men—particularly young men in their late teens and early twenties—might have been too strong a reminder of the soldiers Americans had fought ten years earlier.

Throughout 1956 Cousins continued to bombard readers of the *Saturday Review* with accounts of the Hiroshima Maidens, and after the last of them had returned to Japan he began a sort of annual newsletter in the magazine to keep people informed of the girls' job triumphs, marriages, and babies. (The latter reports are always careful to stress that "the child is in perfect health," thereby helping to counteract some of the rumors that many Hiroshima survivors were giving birth to genetically defective children.) The warmth and family feeling that suffused Cousins's reports of his return visits with the Hiroshima Maidens struck a note of genuine reconciliation and optimism during the late fifties, a time when others harping on Hiroshima were becoming increasingly shrill and anti-American in tone. Cousins was not unaware of that trend. In 1955 he commented, "Here and there . . . serious questions are raised about the justification for the dropping of the bomb. These questions are not to be confused with charges of Communist propagandists who have been attempting since the end of the war to whip up public opinion against the U.S. because of the bombing."[11]

Cousins also gave his readers a lively sense of what the new Hiroshima was all about, and he had the honesty not to romanticize even when this might have suited his temperament and purposes better. In 1949 he was clearly exhilarated by the determined spirit and the rough-and-ready atmosphere of the city. By 1955 he was deeply impressed: "Hiroshima is on the way to becoming one of the most exciting cities, architecturally, in Japan. Already the general outlines are becoming clear. The new park areas have been laid out, the new boulevards are well past the halfway mark, the new and modern civic buildings are being built." By 1970, however, he was a good deal less optimistic: "The hopes for a genuine restructuring of the city crumbled under the

---

[11] *Saturday Review of Literature*, 6 August 1955, p. 31. Among the charges made during the mid-1950s was the assertion that the American bombing of Hiroshima had been a deliberately racist act against Orientals, and that we would never have dropped an atomic bomb on Germany. Interestingly enough, in 1955 the head of the Manhattan Project, General Leslie R. Groves, revealed that precisely the opposite motivation was at work among some of his scientists. The only group at the project that objected to the use of the bomb, he observed, "did not object until after V-E Day. That group was mostly centered around people who were bitterly anti-German and did not appear to feel the same way toward Japan." *New York Times Magazine*, 31 July 1955, p. 9.

weight of too many people, too many things that had to be done in a hurry, too little authority to cope with men who have a compulsion to fill any empty space to overflowing or who think of progress in terms of moving parts. . . . Environmental pollution in Hiroshima is serious and could become critical within a decade." Even when he was being critical, Cousins continued to demonstrate that his real concern was with the present-day Hiroshima and its citizens rather than with their tragic, but irretrievable, past.

Ban-the-Bomb Movements

Meanwhile, the American preoccupation with the symbolic Hiroshima was kept alive by the ban-the-bomb movement of the late-1950s and the furor surrounding the Bikini H-bomb test of 1 March 1954, when a Japanese fishing boat called the *Lucky Dragon* was dusted with radioactive fallout. The physicist and science writer Ralph Lapp published a book concerning this incident, *The Voyage of the Lucky Dragon,* in late 1957. It was excerpted in *Harper's* magazine in January 1958. August 1955, the tenth anniversary of Hiroshima, was greeted with not only a great many magazine articles, but also the publication of Michihiko Hachiya's *Hiroshima Diary,* another eye-witness account which was excerpted in *Look* magazine, and which, despite having been published by the noncommercial University of North Carolina Press, managed to stay on the best-seller list for nine weeks. In June 1960, Fletcher Knebel and Charles W. Bailey's account of Hiroshima, *No High Ground,* was excerpted in *Look* magazine, and in August 1961, Robert Jungk's *Children of the Ashes* was featured in *Redbook.* August 1965 again saw the usual spate of anniversary articles in major magazines, including the *New York Times Magazine* and *Esquire.*

During the late 1950s there was also a good deal of publicity about Claude Eatherly, the so-called "Hiroshima pilot." Eatherly turned to a life of crime allegedly in order to be punished, thus relieving the pervasive guilt he felt over having dropped the atomic bomb. Eatherly was, of course, not the pilot who dropped the bomb on Hiroshima; he had piloted a weather-reconnaissance plane and had been miles away from Hiroshima at the time the bomb was actually dropped. William Bradford Huie, in a book published in 1964, argued rather effectively that Eatherly was more than likely a psychopathic personality who craved the publicity that had surrounded Colonel Tibbets and that his efforts to have himself declared guilt-ridden were simply designed to have him admitted to a VA hospital instead of jail. Nevertheless, Huie's book was by no means a best seller and had little impact on the Eatherly myth—as Huie himself cynically predicted to Eatherly: "The readers of this book will number in thousands, and many of them will believe I was hired by the militarists to smear you. . . . You became what you *are* because by 1960 most of the human race wanted you to *be* the Hiroshima Pilot." [12] In other words, if there had been no Claude Eatherly, Americans would have invented him—in fact, as Huie demonstrated, *did* invent him—as a symbol of American guilt.

The whole issue of American A-bomb guilt, which few people were prepared to face in 1946 and which was shrilly peddled by left-wing groups during the 1950s, was at last made respectable in 1968, when Robert Lifton published *Death in Life*. The book was widely and impressively reviewed and went on to win the science prize at the National Book Awards in 1969 (the same year that Norman Mailer won the arts and letters prize for his *Armies of the Night,* also an anti-war book). Lifton, a psychiatrist, was interested in the psychological reactions of those individuals who had experienced and survived the dropping of an atomic bomb on either Hiroshima or Nagasaki. (As he reminds his readers, Nagasaki was also bombed but everyone always talks about Hiroshima. The reasons are complex and interesting: Hiroshima was first, Hiroshima was more seriously damaged, and Nagasaki has an old and distinguished identity to fall back on aside from being an A-bomb city.)

Death in Life is a sensitive discussion of some of the problems of being an A-bomb survivor: the "survivor-guilt" over having lived when so many (often members of one's own family) died, the angry reaction to this gnawing guilt and the desire to "close off" the whole experience—to get on with life, and the hypochondria, occasioned by the knowledge that radiation can produce illnesses long after the initial exposure. Lifton suggests that many of these survivor reactions can also be found in survivors of Nazi concentration camps or of certain natural disasters, such as earthquakes, floods, or fires, but he goes further to argue that in a sense we are all survivors in the atomic age and are therefore subject to survivor-guilt. Moreover, the desire to close off the experience—a process which Lifton calls "psychic numbing" and

---

[12] William Bradford Huie, *The Hiroshima Pilot* (New York: Pocket Books, 1965), p. 343.

44

claims to have experienced himself as he listened to the stories of survivors—is also said to be a common reaction among the public at large. In his acceptance speech at the National Book Awards, Lifton charged that nuclear weapons had produced "every variety of psychic numbing" to prevent realization of "their brutalizing effects upon human beings."[13]

Unfortunately, much of this analysis smacks of the old Freudian double-bind: if you admit you feel hostile about your mother, you have problems; if you deny you have such hostile feelings, you are repressing them and have problems anyway. Lifton is convinced that everyone feels guilty about Hiroshima, and those who claim not to feel guilty are, instead, accused of psychic numbing. A less psychoanalytic interpretation of present-day American feelings about Hiroshima would run something like this: Yes, Hiroshima continues to be a disturbing component in American attitudes toward Japan. It represents something we did to the Japanese, just as during the war they did certain things to us. Hersey and Cousins effectively humanized the experience for us and made us empathize with the Japanese victims. Robert Jungk, Lifton, and others have tried to stimulate our sense of guilt. Yet in 1971, a Louis Harris poll found that 64 percent of a cross-section of Americans still believed that dropping the atomic bomb had been both "necessary and proper." True, this percentage fell to 53 for individuals aged twenty-one to twenty-four, and to 51 for those aged sixteen to twenty; but even these percentages are high for individuals born after 1945 and having no first-hand experience of World War II. It seems likely that as the World War II generation dies off, the number of Americans who believe the use of the atomic bomb on Japan to have been "necessary and proper" will continue to decline. But it does not stand to reason that just because this percentage decreases, the percentage of people who feel guilt or remorse over Hiroshima will increase. More probably, the passions aroused by this event will simply recede into history, much as the bitterness surrounding the war itself has gradually faded.

---

[13] *New York Times,* 13 March 1969, p. 44.

4

The Legacy of the Occupation

Like the dropping of an atomic bomb on Hiroshima, the American occupation of Japan from 1945 until 1952 left some Americans with ambivalent feelings. At the conclusion of the bitter war there was very little disagreement over the chief objective of the occupation: "To insure that Japan will not again become a menace to the United States or to the peace and security of the world."[1] But the means to be used to achieve this end became a matter of dispute almost instantaneously. Already during the war, as we have seen, there was strong disagreement over whether the emperor should be retained or deposed and tried as a war criminal. That issue was not definitely settled until the American-sponsored Japanese constitution was made public on 6 March 1946 (it did not go into effect until May 1947). Article I stated that "the Emperor shall be the symbol of the State and of the unity of the people, deriving his position from the will of the people with whom resides sovereign power." Nevertheless, many Americans continued to criticize MacArthur for not abolishing the emperor system altogether. In 1949 T. A. Bisson wrote that "Retention of the emperor, even with the drastic modifications effected in his formal constitutional powers, has left the cornerstone of the old structure untouched, and facilitated the oligarchy's efforts to preserve its control."[2]

---

[1] U.S. Department of State, "Basic Initial Post-Surrender Directive," in Jon Livingston, Joe Moore, and Felicia Oldfather, eds., *The Japan Reader,* vol. 2 (New York: Pantheon Books, 1973), p. 7.

[2] T. A. Bisson, *Prospects for Democracy in Japan* (New York: Macmillan, 1949), quoted in ibid., p. 27.

Criticism during the Occupation

Other issues over which debates developed were the extent to which the bureaucracy, government, and business should be purged of wartime leaders, Japanese industry stripped of its "warmaking potential," and reparations paid to former enemies. During the early days of the occupation, its most vociferous critics were American liberals who did not think MacArthur's purges were thorough enough or his attempts to cripple Japanese industry harsh enough. The journalist Mark Gayn, for example, complained that "the infant days of the Occupation was the time to start lopping off political heads, until we had reformed the whole governing body of Japan. We procrastinated, and with each day of delay the Japanese learned more of our weaknesses, and of the ways of using them to thwart our plans." Gayn also noted with approval Edwin Pauley's suggestion to remove from Japan half her capacity for making machine tools, the equipment of twenty shipyards, and all steel capacity in excess of 2,500,000 tons, and he lamented that Japan's huge business combines, the *zaibatsu,* were not to be totally destroyed. "The anti-*zaibatsu* laws were to be allowed to wither by default. Labor was expected to 'modify its demands.' Japan was to be permitted to rebuild her merchant marine. No ceiling was to be put on her industrial expansion." [3]

This liberal passion to purify and pauperize Japan was initially shared by more conservative Americans, who wanted to punish the Japanese for starting the war and, not entirely without ulterior motives, by American businessmen who did not want to see Japan reemerge as a competitive economic power. According to *Fortune* magazine in early 1947, "news and trade papers carried articles by U.S. business leaders denouncing General MacArthur's efforts to rehabilitate the Japanese economy, particularly those parts of it that competed with American manufacturers prior to the war." [4] And the *New York Herald Tribune* of 16 March 1947 reported, "It had been hoped, particularly among textile manufacturers in this country that Japan would be kept down, if not eliminated, as a competitive factor. Ceramic interests are reported to have raised a $200,000 propaganda fund to prevent the Japanese from 'stealing the bread out of American mouths.' " [5]

---

[3] Mark Gayn, *Japan Diary* (New York: William Sloane Associates, Inc., 1948), pp. 501, 6, 504.

[4] R. C. Kramer, "Japan Must Compete," *Fortune,* June 1947, p. 112.

[5] Quoted in Kramer, "Japan Must Compete," p. 112.

But the need to rebuild Japan was compelling: the smashed and leaderless nation was an enormous drain on American funds. In the 12 July 1947 issue of the *Saturday Evening Post,* in an article entitled "Why We're Trading with the Enemy," the case for revitalizing Japan and Germany was made with all the gracelessness and ambivalence typical of the times:

> Are we going to foot the subsistence bills of our former enemies at the rate of $725,000,000 a year? Or are we going to revive their economy, so that the Germans and the Japs at least can pay for their own food and other essentials? Washington, though not happy over the necessity for becoming business partners with the gentry who gave us a sample of their humanity at Buchenwald, Maldémy, and Bataan, think it should be the latter. But Washington wants to revive the German and Japanese economies with an American trigger finger on the controls, for it has the feeling that you can't trust those two countries much farther than you can throw a General Pershing tank.[6]

By 1949 the case for making Japan's economy viable was being put more forcefully. In an editorial in the *Saturday Evening Post,* Helen Mears, who had spent four months in Japan as a member of a labor advisory committee, wrote, "Traditionally Japan has supported around half her population and run her government by profits from foreign trade, overseas enterprises, and services like shipping. Allied policy has destroyed all these sources of income. . . ."[7] And in a long, equally pointed article, *Fortune* magazine wrote, "The tale of Japan is quickly told. Most political and social reforms instituted by the Americans are substantial successes; the economic reforms have been massive failures. Industrial recovery in Japan since the war is the lowest in the world, standing now at about 30 percent of the prewar economy." *Fortune* suggested that Japan be opened to American businessmen wanting to buy and sell goods without the constant interference of the Supreme Commander of the Allied Powers. It attacked SCAP for having commandeered all the best hotels and resorts in Japan for its own use, when Japan, "once a tourist mecca," could again earn much-needed foreign exchange through tourism, and it criticized SCAP for its purge of the

---

[6] Sidney Shalett, "Why We're Trading With the Enemy," *Saturday Evening Post,* 12 July 1947, p. 25.

[7] Helen Mears, "We're Giving Japan 'Democracy,' but She Can't Earn Her Living," *Saturday Evening Post,* 18 June 1949, p. 10.

zaibatsu when "the *zaibatsu* alone, of all major groups in Japan, understood U.S. industrial might and were therefore against war with the United States. But the U.S. Army and the young [SCAP] bureaucrats, ignorant of this history, got rid of 2,000 of the top managers and began to work down into the lower echelons."[8]

Stung to the quick, MacArthur—who usually dismissed all criticism of the occupation and himself as the work of Communists—replied to both of these articles, in the case of the *Fortune* piece with a 6,000-word article of his own. *Fortune* had clearly scored a direct hit. In what is perhaps the shrewdest brief assessment of the occupation yet written, it noted, "What has happened in Japan has been the unexpected marriage of the military mind and the bureaucratic mind; the Army and the New Dealers and socialists who govern Japan, both in Washington and Tokyo, have a natural affinity for the control of their subjects, and other differences have been submerged in the zeal of the two groups to dominate and interfere in the Japanese way of life."[9]

This is certainly not the first time it has been observed that there is a close connection between the authoritarianism of the left and right, but in the context of the American occupation of Japan it goes a long way toward explaining both the occupation itself and the nature of the criticisms that have been leveled against it. MacArthur's men were high-handed; purges were carried out by category, with little regard for what an actual individual might or might not have done to cooperate with the wartime militarists; the Japanese government, the judicial and educational systems, religious institutions, and business enterprises were turned upside down in the name of democracy. One might suppose that once some of the initial bitterness of the war had dissipated, culturally sophisticated Americans would have begun to raise their voices against this root-and-branch approach. And a few of them did. Elizabeth Gray Vining, although she was an admirer of MacArthur and a great believer in his (and her own) mission to democratize Japan, could not help commenting, after she had attended a session of the war crimes trials,

> But as I looked at the eleven judges, able, honorable, distinguished men, some of whom were serving at considerable personal sacrifice, I could not escape the fact that they represented only the victorious nations. There was no Japanese

---

[8] "Two-billion Dollar Failure in Japan: Economic Report on SCAP," *Fortune*, April 1949, pp. 67-73, 204-8.

[9] Ibid., p. 204. For MacArthur's reply, see *Fortune*, June 1949, pp. 74-75, 188-204.

among them. There was not even a neutral, no one from Sweden, Switzerland, Spain, Turkey, or any other nation who had stood outside the conflict. Could a court be impartial and justice be served, when the judges were also the prosecution and the outcome of the trial was known from the beginning? Under ordinary circumstances would we consider a trial fair in which the judge and jury were friends and relatives of the murdered man?

And she quoted Justice Roling, from the Netherlands, as saying "I am afraid to go home. . . . I came here with the Dutch hatred of the Japanese, based on the horrors of war in the Netherlands East Indies and our losses, but after nearly two years I have come to like the Japanese people. They are idealists, and sensitive, and they have something to offer to us westerners, with our emphasis on material things." [10]

But such self-doubt was rare. With the exception of the *Fortune* and *Saturday Evening Post* articles, which were written from the viewpoint of a sort of bluff laissez-faire economics, criticisms of the occupation were invariably more arrogant than the occupation itself. Robert Textor, an avowed anti-Communist who did not want to see the Communist party come to power in Japan, nevertheless argued that "Zaibatsu power must be broken, or democracy in Japan is impossible. . . . It would be folly to put recovery before reform. Even if we did, the Zaibatsu cannot be entrusted with recovery. . . . We should, of course, hope for and work with a democratic middle class. But we should concentrate on the working class." [11] Textor was also upset that under the occupation the American films being imported into Japan were insufficiently propagandistic. "*Oklahoma Kid,* for example, a film which flouts democratic traditions of decency and justice, was not only widely shown, but ballyhooed. *Rhapsody in Blue,* entertaining though it was, certainly did not carry a sufficiently compelling democratic message to warrant the manner in which it was 'premiered' all over western Japan, with local Occupation celebrities as guests of honor." [12] Textor recommended that Hollywood make more documentaries such as *Freedom to Learn, How Laws Are Made,* and *Why Labor Unions,* for the edification of the Japanese.

---

[10] Elizabeth Gray Vining, *Windows for the Crown Prince* (New York: J. B. Lippincott Co., 1952), p. 169.

[11] Robert B. Textor, *Failure in Japan* (New York: John Day Co., 1951), pp. 47, 48, 93.

[12] Ibid., p. 166.

Essentially, such a view is no different from MacArthur's assertion that the Japanese, "measured by the standards of modern civilization . . . would be like a boy of 12 as compared with our development of 45 years. Like any tuitionary period, they were susceptible to following new models, new ideas. You can implant basic concepts there. They were still close enough to origin to be elastic and acceptable to new concepts."[13] The arguments that developed during and after the occupation concerned the choice of ideas to be introduced and the methods to be employed in imposing them on the Japanese. About the basic assumption that the Japanese needed radical reformation there was almost no debate at all—particularly since those who tried to question this assumption were promptly branded fascists.

John Gunther's Assessment

And yet the average American knew and cared very little about any of these ideological struggles. Neither Mark Gayn's *Japan Diary* nor Robert Textor's *Failure in Japan* was a best seller, and aside from the few articles I have mentioned arguing that Japan's economy needed to be set back on its feet, very little was being written about the occupation. When John Gunther arrived in Japan in 1950, he concluded that "before I had been in Tokyo a week I became convinced that the MacArthur story is one of the worst-reported stories in history. By and large, the rank and file of Americans know extremely little about SCAP, its accomplishments and failures, its ambitions, objectives, and ideals."[14] Gunther, of course, intended to rectify this matter, and to a certain extent he did, since his book—published at the height of the controversy over MacArthur's dismissal by Truman—was on the best-seller list for eighteen weeks. But when Gunther set out to research the book, the war in Korea had not yet begun (it erupted while he was in Japan); and although he added a chapter about Korea and, prophetically, another called "MacArthur, Truman, and Formosa," it was not so much

---

[13] U.S. Congress, Senate, *Hearings before the Committee on Armed Services and the Committee on Foreign Relations to Conduct an Inquiry into the Military Situation in the Far East and the Facts Surrounding the Relief of General of the Army Douglas MacArthur from his Assignments in that Area,* part 1, 82nd Congress, 1st session (Washington, D.C.: U.S. Government Printing Office, 1951), p. 312.

[14] John Gunther, *The Riddle of MacArthur* (New York: Harper & Brothers, 1951), p. xiv.

his focus as the focus of his audience that had changed by the time the book appeared. Nevertheless, Gunther's *The Riddle of MacArthur* remains the only unbiased account of the occupation and of MacArthur to reach a wide audience: it was preceded on the best-seller list by John Hersey's adulatory wartime study of MacArthur, *Men on Bataan,* and followed by Charles Willoughby's and Courtney Whitney's paeans and by MacArthur's own self-serving *Reminiscences.*

Gunther, with his imposing reputation and superb access to important individuals, got to interview not only MacArthur and his chief assistants in SCAP, but also the emperor and empress of Japan. He clearly liked MacArthur—"What struck me most was his lightness, humor, and give-and-take"—but this did not prevent him from weighing the general's faults and some of the criticisms leveled against his policies in Japan. Gunther was also impressed with the emperor, whom he sized up as "a personage of powerful will and intelligence, who for good or ill may still play a commanding role in the future of Japan." The emperor told Gunther that he was confident that "[the U.S.'s] democratization of Japan *will* endure after the occupation ends, but that Japanese democracy will be of its own special type, perhaps quite different from that which exists in England or America." [15] This last turns out to be very close to Gunther's own assessment of the occupation. In a sort of wry final catechism, Gunther asks himself a number of questions and then proceeds to answer them:

> *Has MacArthur done a good job?* Of course. *How?* Almost any intelligent dictator can do a good job for a while, given the right material. Simply inspect the record. *Has he done the job he thinks he has done?* Not quite. *Is he sincere in his belief that Japan will become successfully democratized?* Absolutely. He thinks it is democratized already. *Is it?* No. But stupendous progress has been made. *Will it stick?* That is the most important question of all. *Some* of it will stick. . . . A seed has been planted, and something is bound to grow, though we cannot know exactly what. *But on the whole the SCAP record is good, not bad?* Absolutely.[16]

Unfortunately, by the time Gunther's book was published, the public was less interested in these questions than in MacArthur's conduct of the Korean War and in the whys and wherefores of his dismissal, on

15 Ibid., pp. 51, 115.
16 Ibid., pp. 229-31.

11 April 1951, by President Truman. It was already clear in 1950—Gunther accurately describes this in his book—that MacArthur disagreed with the Truman and Acheson policy of fighting a limited war and that he advocated, publicly on occasion, the bombing of Manchuria, the blockading of the China coast, and the "unleashing of Chiang Kai-shek" to create a diversionary landing in south China. Given the outraged reactions of Americans during the late 1960s to actions that might be considered in a similar light—the mining of Haiphong harbor and the bombing of North Vietnam, for example—it seems hard to believe that in 1951 it was Truman who was reviled for his determination to fight a limited war and that MacArthur was hailed as a greatly wronged hero. In the acrimony and heat of the moment—one reporter referred to it as "mass hysteria"—and in view of the bitter debate that developed in Congress about the conduct of the Korean War, it is not surprising that MacArthur's role in the occupation of Japan got very little attention. At most, it was assumed that the occupation was an unblemished success, rendering Truman's abrupt dismissal of MacArthur even more reprehensible. It is also important to bear in mind that on 8 September 1951 the peace treaty with Japan was signed in San Francisco. By the following April the occupation was over and American interest in, and debate over it had become strictly academic.

Academic debate is not unimportant, however, since it is often designed to influence public opinion retroactively: to set the record straight, to justify former behavior, to rewrite history. Up until 1952, it may fairly be said, very few Americans knew much (or cared much) about the occupation, but the general impression was that MacArthur had done a good job in "democratizing Japan." Oddly enough, the way in which MacArthur was removed from his post probably strengthened this impression and helped turn it into a lasting one, since the occupation seemed to be one of the few things on which both MacArthur's detractors and champions could agree. For example, in mid-1951 the *Saturday Review of Literature* conducted a poll of 332 members of the working press who had been reporting the MacArthur recall, and while "by better than six to one the correspondents believe President Truman was right when he recalled General MacArthur" and many were critical of MacArthur's handling of the Korean War, they nevertheless gave him high marks for the occupation of Japan. Among the reporters in Tokyo who participated in the poll, "Some 91 percent say that the occupation was generally successful. . . . A high of 76 percent say that MacArthur's administration went as far toward democratization of Japan as was possible for an occupying power to go." [17] This popular impression of the success of the occupation was undoubtedly enhanced by the highly partisan accounts of Charles Willoughby and Courtney Whitney, and ultimately of Douglas MacArthur himself. All three books made the best-seller list, MacArthur's for better than half a year.

Meanwhile, criticism of the occupation began to appear in the form of academic books, often written by the same individuals who had been involved in the occupation and who had been critical of it then. T. A. Bisson's *Zaibatsu Dissolution in Japan* (1954), for example, is a documented presentation of arguments he was making in 1949 and earlier. A few unbiased books also made their appearance. One of the best was Kazuo Kawai's *Japan's American Interlude* (1960)—a wry and balanced assessment of the occupation by a man in a perfect position to see both sides of the fence. Kawai was a professor of Japanese politics in the United States both before and after the war, but he was born in Japan and spent the war years there, and during the occupation he was editor-in-chief of the *Nippon Times* (today the *Japan Times*), Tokyo's leading English-language daily. In general, however, not many academic studies of any sort dealing with the occupation were forthcoming during the late 1950s and early 1960s. This was partly due to the lamentable condition of the archives and to the restrictions on their use by scholars. The archives, currently housed at the National Records Center, Suitland, Maryland, are unindexed, so that a scholar must have a good idea of what he is looking for before he can even begin; many of the documents are still classified, for reasons purportedly having to do with the sensitivities of the Japanese but most of which seem spurious (a good many Japanese scholars are themselves curious to do research in the archives); and at the present time the archives are totally inaccessible pending the

---

[17] Elmo Roper and Louis Harris, "The Press and the Great Debate," *Saturday Review of Literature,* 14 July 1951, pp. 6, 29. One may well ask why, if the reporters generally favored Truman's position, the general public was so pro-MacArthur. Or, to put it another way, do the mass media have any real influence on public opinion? It should be noted in this connection that the reporters were being asked for their personal opinions: "at least half of the reporters who generally supported Truman on the recall are accredited to newspapers which editorially have been outspoken MacArthur backers." It also seems likely that the reporters, being better informed on this issue than the general public, were simply somewhat ahead of them. Public opinion polls taken during this same period indicated that "the high-water mark of MacArthur popularity was in May. By early June the number of people who thought Truman was right was rising, the number who supported MacArthur falling."

resolution of a dispute about their "ownership" between the Department of the Army and the Chiefs of Staff.

New-Left Criticism

Only in the late 1960s and early 1970s, did a number of younger scholars begin to take an interest in the American occupation of Japan, but with a pronounced ideological bent. Most of them were activists in the anti–Vietnam War movement and believed not only that the United States was the chief aggressor in that war, but also that American imperialism had caused the war in Korea and produced the twenty-year hiatus in our relations with China. As they see it,

> More than two decades ago the Occupation of Japan set the course for the militarist and anti-popular character of American intervention in Asia. . . . With the seizure of Pacific Island bases and the "reverse course" of the Occupation, the banner of an Asian *Pax Americana* was unfurled. A decade earlier Japan had marched through Asia, bombed Pearl Harbor, and carved out an empire justified by anti-Communist politics and the promise of independence and development. That empire was brought to its knees by a combination of American technology, United States Marine human wave assaults, the fire-bombing of Tokyo, nuclear holocaust in Hiroshima and Nagasaki, and heroic efforts of guerrilla fighters in China and other parts of rural Asia. But the end of European and Japanese colonialism brought neither genuine independence nor autonomous development to the nations of "Free Asia." American military and economic power swept in to fill the void left by the departing colonial powers—achieving for America many of the dreams of empire it had denied a vanquished Japan, its rationale then as now the necessity to crush Communist aggression.[18]

An interesting aspect of this passage is its hostility not merely to American actions—the occupation, the fire-bombing of Tokyo, the nuclear bombing of Hiroshima and Nagasaki—but also to Japan and its prewar and wartime policies. (The only people who seem to have behaved splendidly are the heroic guerrilla fighters in China and other parts of rural Asia.) However, such a blanket condemnation of both the United States and Japan tends to create a certain amount of cognitive

---

[18] Edward Friedman and Mark Selden, *America's Asia: Dissenting Essays on Asian-American Relations* (New York: Vintage Books, 1971), p. xi.

dissonance in the minds of true believers. If prewar Japan was a fascist state, can the United States be wholly condemned for fighting World War II? (This question becomes even more problematical for leftists with regard to Hitler's Germany.) One way, but a very strange way, out of this dilemma is the route chosen by Noam Chomsky. Chomsky has concluded that Japan was, in fact, not to blame for its behavior in China during the 1930s, nor for its decision to bomb Pearl Harbor, because it was already a victim of American and European imperialism and was merely trying to defend itself. In other words, the United States was the true aggressor nation: "[Japan] was in no position to tolerate a situation in which India, Malaya, Indochina, and the Philippines erected tariff barriers favoring the mother country, and could not survive the deterioration in its very substantial trade with the United States and the sharp decline in China trade. It was, in fact, being suffocated by the American and British and other Western imperial systems, which quickly abandoned their lofty liberal rhetoric as soon as the shoe began to pinch." [19] Interestingly enough, part of Chomsky's argument concerning the reasons for Japan's aggression in the 1930s is a perfectly acceptable one in academic circles; however, it is usually associated with conservative scholars who argue that America's insistence on unconditional surrender was too moralistic and that the occupation was too punitive. But ideology produces strange bedfellows. Ambassador Joseph Grew, who was reviled by liberals during and after the war as a Japan-lover and a supporter of the "old guard," becomes a hero in Chomsky's eyes for having tried to reach an accommodation with the Japanese in Asia up until the moment of Pearl Harbor.

Another scholar on the left who has great difficulties in reconciling his dislike of the prewar Japanese with his dislike of American occupation policies is Richard H. Minear, the author of *Victors' Justice* (1971). Dedicating his book to "the many Americans whose opposition to the war in Indochina has made them exiles, criminals, or aliens in their own land," Minear makes it clear that his attack on the Tokyo war crimes trials is politically motivated: "The war in Indochina changed [me]. For one thing, it soon became obvious from my study of the American involvement there that very little about American policy was right. Could American policy be enlightened regarding Japan when it was so

---

[19] Noam Chomsky, *American Power and the New Mandarins* (New York: Pantheon Books, 1969), pp. 191-92.

benighted about Vietnam? Very likely not." [20] However, to attack the war-crimes trials as a brand of "victors' justice," chiefly perpetrated by the United States, poses problems for someone who believes that war crimes were committed in Vietnam for which he would like to see U.S. officials tried. Therefore, Minear backs away from the implications of his study that all war crimes except those covered by the Geneva and The Hague conventions are likely to result in purely political trials. For example, he would like to see "two American presidents and their civilian and military advisors" be held responsible for military policies in Vietnam such as free-fire zones and saturation bombing. Only when it comes to a Bertrand Russell type of war crimes trial for the United States does Minear reluctantly conclude that he must demur. "A tribunal convened today to consider these issues might come closer to the truth than did the Tokyo tribunal after World War II. That would be child's play. But how close is close enough?" [21] Nor do Minear's conclusions about the Tokyo trials lead him to a completely Chomsky-like position concerning the people tried: "The Tokyo tribunal dismissed the claim that the Japanese government had been motivated by considerations of self-defense. It is my contention that considerations of self-defense played an important role. But my brief for Japan's prewar policies stops there. Many Japanese acts on the continent of Asia before and during the war are as repugnant to me as current American acts in Indochina." [22] What, then, does he think Americans should have done with Japan's militarists? "Perhaps," he concludes, "summary executions might have been preferable"; but then, because this sounds even more lawless than the lawlessness he has been inveighing against, he suggests that perhaps nothing should have been done. In a remark he no doubt regrets in the days since Watergate, he observes that "For defeated leaders the fact of defeat itself is surely of greater moment than any subsequent punishment." [23]

I refer to these muddled rewritings of history not because they have had any great influence on American public opinion concerning the occupation of Japan—they have not—but because they do signal an

---

[20] Richard H. Minear, *Victors' Justice: The Tokyo War Crimes Trial* (Tokyo: Charles Tuttle Co., 1972), p. xii. (Published by Princeton University Press in the United States.)

[21] Ibid., p. xi.

[22] Ibid., p. x.

[23] Ibid., p. 180.

interesting change in American left-wing thought. The early attacks on the occupation share with the later ones a simultaneous distrust of American policy and of the Japanese, who are invariably characterized as devious and authoritarian. But the proposed liberal solution in those early postwar days was *more* American interference—more trust-busting, more purges, more land reform, more draconian measures. Today, in the wake of the Vietnam War, there are often bitter liberal attacks on American policies in the Far East, but there is no proposed solution other than that we should simply "stop it," or "get out." As Henry Kissinger recently observed, this is really a new form of isolationism. "The old isolationism [of the '20s and '30s, primarily a conservative phenomenon] was based on the proposition that we were too good for this world; the new isolationism [is] based on the proposition that we're not good enough for it." [24] During the 1940s, by contrast, Americans managed to feel strongly enough about something called "democracy" to help defeat the Axis powers and to attempt "democratizing" Japan. In retrospect, our goals may not seem quite as selfless and pure as we then believed them to be, but it is hardly likely that they were (and are) as black as some would paint them now.

Popular American opinion about the occupation of Japan seems to lean toward some such middle view. On the whole, Americans believe that the occupation brought some much needed democratic changes to postwar Japan, but they never expected to see Japan turned into a carbon copy of the United States; in fact, many tourists now resent that Japan has become so westernized. Once the occupation had ended, most Americans took the rather healthy attitude some parents take toward grown children: we have done what we could; the rest is up to you. If, within a few years of the occupation, Japan had gone either Communist or Fascist, there doubtless would have been a wave of soul-searching in the United States. Was it our fault? Where did we go wrong? But instead Japan developed one of the fastest growing economies in the world; American tourism there blossomed; a vast array of high-quality, Japanese-made goods began to flow into the United States; and we became rather proud of our former protégé. The occupation must have been a success, most Americans reasoned, if it accomplished (or at least did not prevent) all that.

---

24 Interview with James Reston, *New York Times,* 13 October 1974, p. 35.

5

The Sexual Nexus

Toward the end of the war, "Pappy" Boyington, who had been a prisoner of war since January 1944, was chatting with one of the Japanese interpreters in his camp whom he called "Jimmy." Boyington asked him,

> "How do you think the Americans and Japanese are going to make out when they intermarry after the war's over?" [Jimmy] leaned back on the legs of his chair, placing his feet in anything but true Japanese fashion on top of the table between us, thought awhile, then started talking: "I believe Japanese women would make wonderful mates for the American men, but I don't think that the American women could stand the Japanese men." "Why do you think that way?" And what he told me made sense, and is just exactly the way it turned out after the war. Jimmy said: "The Japanese woman is very affectionate, and is devoted to her husband. Yet she remains in the background, and doesn't try to run everything. But our men, I know, would never be able to keep up with the American women." [1]

One reason, of course, why it worked out in the way "Jimmy" predicted is that the American occupation brought far more men than women to Japan, so the bulk of the meetings that occurred were between American men and Japanese women. Many Japanese women had also lost husbands during the war; all Japanese were desperately poor during the first years after the war; and the army of occupation, far away from their own wives and girlfriends, had access to food and other scarce items through the P.X. Thus a variety of motivations brought American

---

[1] "Pappy" [Colonel Gregory] Boyington, *Baa Baa Black Sheep* (New York: G. P. Putnam's Sons, 1958), p. 309.

men and Japanese women together. The Japanese also made it relatively easy for American men to gain access to certain women. Fearful at first that the occupation army would commit indiscriminate rape, and with a long tradition of maintaining houses of prostitution near their own army bases, the Japanese rapidly set up houses of prostitution exclusively for the American GIs. In May 1946, according to Mark Gayn, there were 668 known brothels in Tokyo alone, with a total of 8,000 women.[2] The rapidity with which fraternization between Japanese women and occupation soldiers began to occur is also illustrated by two *New York Times* cartoons dating from 30 September 1945.

In 1946, there were an estimated 465,000 American soldiers stationed in Japan to disarm troops and begin the occupation. This number dwindled rapidly, however, until by 1948, there were only an estimated 125,000 occupation forces. With the outbreak of the Korean War, the numbers increased again to between 210,000 and 260,000 throughout the early fifties. Not until 1957 did the numbers of American troops in Japan fall below 100,000. Thereafter, they declined steadily until by 1959 there were 58,000; by 1965, 40,000; by 1971, 30,500; and by January of 1974, 19,000. Adding up these annual figures and dividing by two (the number of years the average GI spent in Japan), one comes up with an estimate of approximately 2 million American men who have lived in Japan as members of the armed forces. And this figure does not include civilian members of SCAP, the numbers of Korean War troops who were sent to Japan for R and R, or the Navy men whose ships have called at Japanese ports for shorter or longer periods of time.

Given such an influx, it is not surprising that by 1955 an estimated 20,000 American GIs had married Japanese girls, even though such marriages were at first forbidden by MacArthur and were never made easy. The number of men who had a serious affair, a liaison, or something much briefer with a Japanese girl is obviously much larger. The novelist George Stewart once estimated that for every book published in the United States, there are at least ten that are rejected; for every manuscript rejected, there are ten completed but not sent out; for every manuscript completed but not sent out, there are ten started but not completed; and for every manuscript started but not completed, there are ten thought about but never started. By means of this geometric progression, Stewart calculated that every man, woman, and child in

---

[2] Mark Gayn, *Japan Diary* (New York: William Sloane Associates, Inc., 1948), p. 234.

"If it wasn't I ain't fraternizin', I'd want to know who's he."

Reprinted with permission from the **New York Times Magazine**

"You sure there ain't been no jitterbugging GI's hanging out around here?"

Reprinted with permission from the **New York Times Magazine**

the United States has at some time thought about writing, or actually written, a book. Similarly, for every GI who married a Japanese girl there must have been ten who seriously thought about it, and for every one of those there must have been another ten who may not have thought about marriage but who were seriously infatuated. What is there about Japanese women that could produce such a phenomenon, and what effect has it had on the attitudes of Americans toward Japan?

American Men and Japanese Women

From almost the onset of contact between the two countries, there has been a fascination on the part of American men with Japanese women. There is a legend that the first American envoy to Japan, Townsend Harris, had a liaison with a beautiful geisha, although less romantic versions of the story maintain she was merely a washerwoman and a prostitute, and Harris, who kept a voluminous journal, never mentions her at all. Lafcadio Hearn, however, married a Japanese woman of a reputable, if destitute, samurai family, and while the marriage did not begin as a romance—Hearn needed someone to cook and care for him, and her family had no better prospects for their daughter given their financial situation—it grew into a true union of East and West. "How sweet the Japanese woman is!" Hearn wrote to his friend and fellow Japanologist, the Englishman Basil Chamberlain. "All the possibilities of the race for goodness seem to be concentrated in her. It shakes one's faith in some Occidental doctrines. If this be the result of suppression and oppression—then these are not altogether bad. On the other hand, how diamond-hard the character of the American woman becomes under the idolatry of which she is the subject." [3] Later, in his book *Japan: An Attempt at Interpretation,* he wrote:

> Perhaps no such type of woman will appear again in this world for a hundred thousand years: the conditions of industrial civilization will not admit of her existence. . . . Only a society under extraordinary regulation and regimentation, —a society in which all self-assertion was repressed, and self-sacrifice made a universal obligation, —a society in which personality was clipped like a hedge, permitted to bud and bloom from within, never from without, —in short, only a society founded upon ancestor-worship, could have produced it. . . . Trans-

---

[3] Elizabeth Stevenson, *Lafcadio Hearn* (New York: The Macmillan Co., 1961), p. 228.

planted successfully it cannot be: under a foreign sun its forms revert to something altogether different, its colors fade, its perfume passes away. The Japanese woman can be known only in her own country.[4]

Hearn, like most Western men, was deeply attracted to what he called the "moral charm" of Japanese women—what we today might call their character—but he was not immune to their physical allure. He thought them "slight and dainty, with admirable little hands and feet," and while their eyes and eyelids might seem strange at first, "yet they are often very charming. . . . Even if she cannot be called handsome, according to Western standards, the Japanese woman must be confessed pretty, —pretty like a comely child; and if she is seldom graceful in the Occidental sense, she is at least in all her ways incomparably graceful: her every motion, gesture, or expression being, in its own Oriental manner, a perfect thing." The same year this was published, Puccini's Lieutenant Benjamin Franklin Pinkerton first began singing about his Cho-Cho-San, "Delicate and fragile as blown glass, in stature, in bearing she resembles some figure on a painted screen, but as, from her background of glossy lacquer, with a sudden movement she frees herself; like a butterfly she flutters and settles with such quiet grace that a madness seizes me to pursue her, even though I might damage her wings." And, as he watches her change from her wedding-kimono into something more comfortable: "With squirrel-like movements she shakes the knots loose and undoes them! To think that this little toy is my wife! My wife! But she displays such grace that I am consumed by a fever of sudden desire!"

I cite these early paeans by Westerners to Japanese female charm and beauty to demonstrate that the phenomenon did not originate during the occupation. It is obvious from Hearn's comment about the diamond-hard character of the American woman, that Japanese women with their compliance, gentleness, and obedience have long struck a responsive chord in men who are used to self-assertive, brash, independent American girls. But the postwar years may have heightened this American male responsiveness. This was the period of what Betty Friedan has so aptly called "the feminine mystique," when American women were being urged to stay at home having babies and being good housewives. Friedan considers this a bill of goods that was somehow foisted onto gullible

---

[4] Lafcadio Hearn, *Japan: An Attempt at Interpretation* (New York: The Macmillan Co., 1924 [first published 1904]), p. 394.

women; she does not stop to analyze that powerful social forces may have been at work shaping the needs of both men and women. In all known societies the end of a devastating war brings an upsurge in the birthrate, an expression of both the psychological urge of individuals to forget the ugly fact of death and the social system's need to replenish itself. Men and women want, and society needs, a period of relative quiet in which traditional values can reassert themselves. In the United States (and also in Europe and Japan) the immediate postwar years saw the emergence of a generation of parents—those just entering their twenties as well as those somewhat older who had postponed marriage until after the war—who deeply wanted the peaceful, bourgeois existence that the war had denied them. (They raised a generation of children who, in turn, rebelled against this lifestyle of their parents and sought out the violence of campus revolutions.) American housewives during the late 1940s and early '50s adopted an ethos that both they and their husbands found appealing, but it was not nearly as deeply engrained in American women as in their Japanese counterparts. When American GIs reached Japan and found women who brought them their slippers, fixed them tea, and drew them a hot bath—all without being asked— they thought they had arrived in a paradise for men.

Michener's *Sayonara*

The best seller that gave classic expression to all this was James Michener's *Sayonara*. Michener, who himself married a Japanese woman in 1955, has his novel end unhappily—the narrator, Major Lloyd Gruver, is ultimately separated from his great love, the Takarazuka girl Hana-ogi, and presumably goes back to his American girlfriend, the attractive but somewhat cold and domineering daughter of a general. A secondary romance in the book, between Private Joe Kelly and his Japanese wife Katsumi, ends even more disastrously when the army refuses him permission to take her back to the United States and they commit double-suicide. Yet the unhappy endings did not detract from the great success of the book, probably because they enabled readers, in a variety of ways, to have their cake and eat it too. Men who had been in Japan could relive their own bittersweet romances with Japanese girls but at the same time reaffirm their good sense in having left the girls behind. For men who had never been to Japan it was a sort of wish-fulfillment book of what it might have been like to love a "golden-skinned beauty."

67

American women—who are cruelly caricatured throughout the book—were instead made to identify with the soft, pliable, beautiful Japanese heroine, and they were subtly invited to learn something from her appealing ways. At the same time, the heroine's reasons for giving up her American lover are enough to please the most fastidious women's liberationist: Hana-ogi is a great dancer who has devoted years to the study of her art, and her dedication to her profession and her audience must come before her personal happiness. Finally, American women could identify with Eileen, the general's daughter, who ultimately gets the hero and who—we are left to understand—has become more understanding and less pushy as a result of having witnessed his Japanese affair.

Michener's portrait of Japanese womanhood is calculated to touch all of these bases. The comforting, housewifely ways are primarily depicted in the rather homely Katsumi:

> Katsumi was alone, singing to herself as she prepared dinner. I sat on the floor and watched her time-christened movements over the charcoal stoves that Japanese women have used for centuries. For them there were no can openers, no frozen foods. Each item was laboriously prepared by hand and as Katsumi did this ancient work she hummed old songs and it seemed to me that she grew lovelier each day.... I could immediately visualize fat little Katsumi Kelly the other night, taking her sore and defeated husband into the bath and knocking the back of his neck and getting him his kimono and quietly reassuring him that her love was more important than whatever Lt. Col. Calhoun Craford had done to him, and I saw runty, sawed-off Joe Kelly coming back to life as a complete man and I had great fear . . . that Eileen Webster would not be able or willing to do that for her man. Oh, she would be glad to storm in and fight it out with Lt. Col. Craford, or she would take a job and help me earn enough so that I could tell Lt. Col. Craford to go to hell, or she could do a million other capable things; but I did not think she could take a wounded man and make him whole, for my mother in thirty years of married life had never once, so far as I knew, done for my father the simple healing act that Katsumi Kelly had done for her man the other night.[5]

The Japanese woman's strength of character is depicted in the beautiful Hana-ogi:

---

[5] James A. Michener, *Sayonara* (Greenwich, Conn.: Fawcett Publications Inc., 1964 [copyright 1953, 1954]), pp. 97, 106.

There was a firmness about her mouth when she said this and I was surprised, for I had to come to look upon her as the radiant symbol of all that was best in the Japanese woman: the patient accepter, the tender companion, the rich lover, but when Hana-ogi displayed her iron will I reflected that throughout the generations of Japanese women there had also been endlessly upon them this necessity to be firm, not to cry, not to show pain. They had to do a man's work, they had to bear cruel privations, yet they remained the most feminine women in the world. . . . I concluded that no man could comprehend women until he had known the women of Japan with their unbelievable combination of unremitting work, endless suffering and boundless warmth—just as I could never have known even the outlines of love had I not lived in a little house where I sometimes drew back the covers of my bed upon the floor to see there the slim golden body of the perpetual woman.[6]

And, for contrast, we have the American woman:

I looked around me at the faces of my countrywomen. They were hard and angular. They were the faces of women driven by outside forces. They looked like my successful and unhappy mother, or like powerful Mrs. Webster, or like the hurried, bereft faces you see on a city street anywhere in America at four-thirty any afternoon. They were efficient faces, faces well made up, faces showing determination, faces filled with a great unhappiness. They were the faces of women whose men had disappointed them. Possibly these harsh faces in the Osaka P.X. bore an unusual burden, for they were surrounded each day with cruel evidence that many American men preferred the softer, more human face of some Japanese girl like Katsumi Kelly.[7]

Aside from its paeans to Japanese womanhood, Michener's *Sayonara* is also in some respects the first postwar travel guide to Japan. In the course of his story he describes rather accurately the etiquette and pleasures of the Japanese bath, the training and performances of the Takarazuka girls, Japanese foods such as raw fish and vinegared rice, tempura, and sukiyaki (as well as how to pronounce them correctly), the Osaka puppet theater, woodblock prints, a few elements of the Japanese language, including some very amusing examples of the pidgin Japanese-English used by interracial couples, and suicide and its role in Japanese society. A 1950s soldier or tourist in Japan who read nothing

---

[6] Ibid., pp. 127-28.
[7] Ibid., pp. 120-21.

else about the country but Michener's *Sayonara* would have gained a sympathetic understanding of Japanese culture from it. Such an understanding was all the more effectively elicited because Michener assumed that many of his readers probably started the book with certain wartime prejudices. Consequently the narrator, Major Lloyd Gruver, is made to share these prejudices at the outset: "I'd been through the place [Japan] and it never impressed me much. Dirty streets, little paper houses, squat men and fat round women. . . . How can our men—good average guys— how can they marry these yellow girls? In '45 I was fighting the Japs. Now my men are marrying them." [8] It is, of course, Gruver's love affair with Hana-ogi that brings about his own conversion—just as thousands of real-life soldiers softened their attitudes toward Japan because they fell in love with Japanese girls.

American Women and Japanese Men

If the idealization of Japanese women helped Japan's postwar image, the sexual image of her men produced more contradictory results. To begin with, there was simply not enough contact between Japanese men and American women to produce a comparable effect. Also, most American women in Japan during the immediate postwar years were either in uniform themselves or civilian employees of the occupation, and it is not likely that a man from a defeated country would have dared to make advances to a woman so clearly above him in status. Nor is it likely, had one dared, that his advances would have been accepted; most single American women in occupied Japan were there partly hoping to meet and marry an American serviceman. But even if greater opportunities had existed, romantic attachments between Japanese men and American women seem to involve very different stereotypes.

One surprising best seller of the postwar period—surprising because it was modestly published by a university press—was a sort of female real-life *Sayonara*: Gwen Terasaki's *Bridge to the Sun*. Gwen Terasaki was born Gwen Harold in Johnson City, Tennessee. In 1930, when she was twenty-three, she came to Washington, D. C. to visit her aunt, and at a Japanese embassy reception she met Hidenari [Terry] Terasaki, then private secretary to Japanese Ambassador Debuchi. The young couple fell in love and were married a year later. Terasaki spoke good

---

[8] Ibid., pp. 7, 11.

70

English (he had studied for a year at Brown University) and was obviously a rather sophisticated Japanese, destined for a career in his country's diplomatic service. Yet his wife was attracted not only by his "western" traits but by his Japanese qualities. When they were still dating, she would occasionally go out with other men although "this made Terry furious. . . . His attitude ranged from wonder to muted rage. I did not stop going out with other men, but I realized that whoever married Terry would have to get her way by indirect means; he was a forceful, dominating person. I felt the magnetism of his dark, intelligent eyes and was a little disturbed." After they were married, "for all his ideas and ebullience of sentiment when we were alone, Terry was not only a true Japanese outwardly but a formal Japanese at that. If he met me on the street, he would remove his hat and say, 'How do you do, my beloved wife'. . . . During all our married life he never once entered my bedroom without knocking." Even toward the end of their 19-year marriage (Terasaki died at a relatively young age due to a stroke), his wife noted, "His long years of training still inhibited him from expressing affection in words. Over the years this was changing slowly but something in his formal nature still recoiled at acknowledging emotion." [9]

Obviously, such men have their attractions for certain women, and the type—decisive, somewhat arrogant, perhaps a little cruel—is an exact match for the ideal-type Japanese woman who meekly waits to carry out his every wish. But whereas a compliant Japanese woman can greatly delight even a nonmasterful man, an arrogant man is not so likely to strike a responsive chord in all women. This may be one reason why the sexual attractions of the Japanese male stereotype are not as highly touted in the United States as those of the female stereotype. Nevertheless, the Japanese male stereotype can exercise a strong fascination on American women, as was made clear when a long panoramic novel called *The Time of the Dragons* hit the best-seller list for some sixteen weeks in 1958 and also did well as a Literary Guild selection.

Alice Ekert-Rotholz, the author of *The Time of the Dragons,* was an unknown German writer at the time her book was published in the United States in a good translation by Richard and Clara Winston. She had lived in Bangkok from 1939 until 1952, and she set her novel in turbulent prewar and wartime Asia. Her story begins on 7 December 1925 with a party at the home of the Norwegian consul in Shanghai,

---

[9] Gwen Terasaki, *Bridge to the Sun* (Chapel Hill: University of North Carolina Press, 1957), pp. 7, 20, 40, 252.

71

and ends in the mid-1950s in Paris. Much of the novel revolves around the fortunes of the Norwegian consul's family—he has three daughters: one by a French wife, one by a Norwegian wife, and one by a Chinese mistress—yet the mainspring of the action in the book is a young, well-born Japanese, Baron Akiro Matsubara. The reader first meets Matsubara when he attends Consul Wergeland's party and is insulted by an American businessman.

> At that moment of deadly disgrace Akiro . . . developed the Japanese X-ray eye. That penetrating, disillusioned keenness was born of hatred. It was a hatred preserved by a phenomenal memory and by the Japanese principle of education, which held vengeance to be a noble masculine duty. Revenge of an insult was one aspect of *giri*, the duty that every Japanese owes to his family, the state, and the Tenno, the Son of Heaven. As young Baron Matsubara, on his first night abroad, stared at the tactless American, he felt for the first time the fullness of his powers of concentration. Here too was something basically and typically Japanese, an odd peculiarity of that inscrutable nation: that a cruel shock did not make a Japanese cynical or indifferent toward his enemies. It intensified his vitality.[10]

By the 1930s, Baron Matsubara has become a lieutenant, later a major, in the Kempeitai. His wife, whom he despises for not having borne him any sons, commits suicide to save face. Meanwhile Matsubara is back in China trying to crack a complex spy network which transmits information about Japanese economic and war installations in China to the allies. Vivica Wergeland, the Norwegian daughter of the now dead consul, is an unwitting courier in this spy network and is arrested by Baron Matsubara, who years before had once met and admired her mother. Matsubara questions the young girl and treats her cruelly, but at the same time he is deeply attracted to her. Finally, when she is almost unconscious,

> Matsubara Akiro, who had hitherto overcome erotic temptations with the aid of Zen discipline, stood before the foreign girl and repeated, "Kino do'ku, kino do'ku" [which, the author tells us, means "Oh, this poisonous feeling"]. He whispered more and more shrilly and hastily; the savagery of the Japanese lover was coming to the fore. He must enjoy this bundle of glory, sex, and stupidity at once, this very second, so that he would be able to toss it aside afterward. For after the embrace

---

[10] Alice Ekert-Rotholz, *The Time of the Dragons* (New York: The Viking Press, 1958), p. 29.

there came, in due order, first purifying regret at the loss of masculine force and discipline, then brutal indifference toward the giver of pleasure. The episode ended for the Japanese man by his returning home to the "pure room," where the last remnant of unstilled desire was cleared away by the chastening powers of the mind.[11]

Matsubara does not actually rape the girl, but he comes mighty close.

During the postwar period Matsubara spends five years in prison as a war criminal, while Vivica Wergeland marries an American doctor whom she meets in China. She is still deeply disturbed by her wartime experiences and somewhat dissatisfied with her marriage to the good-hearted but square American, who is by now a doctor stationed in occupied Japan. One day, at the Fujiya Hotel in the resort town of Miyanoshita, Vivica meets Matsubara again, recognizes him as her wartime torturer, and yet feels strangely drawn to him. He invites her to visit his country house in Karuizawa, and one summer evening after a boring army party she does so. Matsubara correctly senses why she has come and shows her into his Japanese tea house, where he is just about to ravish her—this time, with her consent—when he opens the locket around her neck and sees a picture of her young son.

> Major-san's face contorted in a grief that only a Japanese woman would have understood. This package of beauty and timid sensuality had given to another man something Matsubara Akiro had hungered for all his life—a *son!* . . . Separated from Vivica by the greatest of gulfs, Akiro studied the photograph and the inscription and then returned it without a word to the quivering young woman. Vivica was so shaken by passion that she could scarcely breathe. Tears filled her nymph's eyes; with all her might she repressed the insane impulse to throw herself at the feet of this demon lover who unexpectedly burned and froze—to throw herself at his feet and beg for caresses that were like winds in the desert of unfulfilled desire, like poppy petals brushing over shivering skin, like flashes of lightning cutting into the slumber of the senses, like whiplashes, one moment volcanic fire and the next as gentle as the veiled moon and the fragrance of dying flowers. But such raptures were not for a young mother, to whom every man owed only respect and admiration. From one fateful moment to the next the climate in the pure, lovely room had utterly changed. Abruptly a passionate lover had become a Japanese moralist. Matsubara Akiro had not dreamed that this flowery

---

[11] Ibid., p. 295.

consolation girl, whom he had alternately adored and wished to destroy for years, was already a stroller in the golden garden of motherhood, a dreamer forgetful of her duties. Such a one was no concern of his.[12]

We last see Matsubara in Paris—enjoying once again the scenes of his youth, and visiting a gallery where some paintings by Vivica are on display. (It has been made clear throughout the book that despite the Major's cruelty, he is also highly cultivated and artistic.) The final words of the book are: "His passion for her had been a moment of glory between waking and sleeping, between birth and death. Before and afterward there had been only the precisely determined duties laid down by Shintoism and the Japanese family system. Like the Imperial Chrysanthemum, duties were not subject to time's mutability. Matsubara Akiro had been born into this order, and he had no quarrel with it. Tomorrow morning his plane would be leaving for Peiping [where he hopes to promote trade and restore the fortunes of his *zaibatsu* family]."

American Men and Japanese Men

Although by no means great literature, *The Time of the Dragons,* like *Sayonara,* was extremely popular and demonstrates the existence of a stereotype—in this case of the Japanese male demon lover, who is cruel, imperious, quixotic. It is a type destined to appeal to masochistic women—and also to certain men. For although it is seldom noted in scholarly books about Japan, it is an interesting fact that since the war Japan has had a strong attraction for male homosexuals. It is difficult to say precisely why this should be so. The psychologically trained anthropologist George De Vos has suggested it is merely because homosexuality in Japan is less of a taboo and therefore the homosexual is less stigmatized and his life is less compartmentalized. A good many Japanese homosexuals also have stable marriages and children, and their homosexual affairs are treated no differently from liaisons with bar-girls or geisha. According to one American homosexual living in Japan, some Japanese wives accept a homosexual lover for their husbands more easily than a relationship with a bar hostess because there is less chance of losing her own position or of having her home broken up.[13]

---

[12] Ibid., p. 436.

[13] As quoted in Ronald Bell, ed., *The Japan Experience* (New York: Weatherhill Inc., 1973), p. 217.

Homosexuality also has a long history in Japan. As Oliver Statler noted in his best seller *Japanese Inn,*

> love between men was neither new nor uncommon in Japan [at the time it was first commented on by a Dutch traveler in 1691]. . . . Centuries before, it had flourished in the quickly spreading Buddhist temples and monasteries, whose members were forbidden the love of women. . . . Then it had spread to the warrior class, among whom it was frequently proclaimed that love for a woman was an effeminate failing. In both cloister and barracks, the love of man for man was more than mere sensual gratification. Ideally, at least, it was based on a lasting relation of loyalty and devotion. However, as has frequently been chronicled, sex does not always live up to the ideal. The world's oldest profession had its male as well as its female practitioners, and the all-male Kabuki theatre was, for a time, chiefly a showcase for the charms of pretty young men.[14]

The existence, in Japan, of "pretty young men" is no doubt another reason why American homosexuals are attracted to the country. Some homosexuals are drawn to the Baron Matsubara type, but others prefer the slim, beardless, high-cheekboned, aesthetic-looking youths. The fact that such young men are attractive to foreign homosexuals, coupled with the existence in Japan of such "effeminate" arts as flower-arranging and the tea ceremony, which are often practiced by men, has caused some American men to believe that all Japanese males are somehow unmasculine. (This notion may have contributed to the readiness of American soldiers to go after Japanese women: they did not see Japanese men as sexual rivals.)

Like their British counterparts in certain Arab countries, a number of American homosexuals who fell in love with Japan for personal reasons stayed on to become experts on the language and the culture. Some became translators of Japanese poetry and novels, others became experts on Kabuki or *Noh* or on the Japanese film. Over the years they have performed an enormously valuable service in introducing traditional Japanese arts and aesthetics to Americans. It is fair to say, however, that in doing so they have been guided by their own tastes and have often emphasized the subtle, the hypersensitive, the perverse, so that many Americans have absorbed vaguely homosexual connotations from Japanese culture.

---

14 Oliver Statler, *Japanese Inn* (New York: Random House, 1961), p. 159.

In general, it is the image of Japanese women that was and remains highly favorable among American men. American women found the image of the Japanese woman somewhat appealing during the 1950s, when they were trying to approximate a similar lifestyle themselves. More recently, especially with the birth of the women's liberation movement, the image of Japanese womanhood is likely to make American women acutely uncomfortable, if not furious. Kate Millett, who spent two years in Japan in the early 1960s, began by enjoying her freedom as a foreign woman who could sit up and chat with the men, "until my growing realization that the woman who waited upon me with bowed head was after all my sister began to ruin the taste of my sake and contaminate the flavor of the sashimi." [15]

American women have always been ambivalent toward Japanese men—occasionally seeing in them cruel and masterful demon lovers, but more commonly viewing them as small, rather effeminate creatures. For American men, the cruel Japanese male stereotype is more likely to derive from wartime imagery than from sexual fantasies, but the opposite notion of effeminacy probably does derive from the sexual predilections of a small group of American homosexuals who have conveyed this image in their writings, as well as from the way certain aspects of traditional Japanese culture strike the ordinary American male.

I would not want to claim too much influence for the sexual nexus between Japanese and American men and women, but I do think it colors and gives emotional force to many more visible events. I also think it has contributed to the climate of ambivalence that often pervades relations between the two countries. American men are deeply attracted to Japanese women but, unless they are homosexuals, they are rather put off by Japanese men, whom they tend to see in terms of either the effeminate or the cruel stereotype. American women tend to reject Japanese women, whom they alternately pity and envy, and unless they are somewhat masochistic, they are generally completely unmoved by Japanese men. The fact that American women are not drawn to *either* Japanese women or men may help to explain why the field of Japanese studies attracts relatively few female scholars. On the other hand, many American women (and also aesthetically inclined men) have been attracted by the artistic side of Japanese life—the ceramics, painting, sculpture, architecture, and gardens—and this has proved to be an important bridge between the two countries.

---

[15] Kate Millett, "A Personal Discovery," *MS.* magazine, March 1973, p. 57.

6
The Cultural Nexus

American men fell in love with Japanese women almost from the day the marines landed, but the American infatuation with Japanese culture—particularly with traditional Japanese culture—was a bit slower in developing. In its 18 February 1946 issue, *Life* devoted a page of pictures and text to the Japanese tea ceremony, but its grudging commentary was a far cry from the praise that would later be lavished on this ancient ritual: "The Japs still preen themselves, as they did 500 years ago, on the studied etiquette with which they serve and drink tea. . . . Perfected at a time when Japan was swept by civil war and was on the threshold of its era of total isolationism [circa 1550], it trained the Japs in introspection, meditation, frugality, restraint and poverty, the isolationist qualities which made Japan the kind of nation it is today."

Oliver Statler, who arrived in Japan during the occupation, tells how the Minaguchi-ya, the setting for his book *Japanese Inn,* was placed on limits for occupationaires, but every faucet in the place was neatly labeled by the American authorities, "This water is unfit for drinking or brushing teeth." American guests were also obliged to bring their own food, partly because MacArthur did not want his men depriving the Japanese of what little food there was, but also because "the Army Medical Department . . . devised a propaganda barrage to convince us that Japanese food, because of the human fertilizer used to grow it, was so unsanitary as to be almost instantly fatal."[1]

Occupationaires no doubt learned *something* about Japanese culture; many men dutifully sent home sets of Noritake china and glass-encased Hakata dolls to their families in the States, but the regulations

---

[1] Oliver Statler, *Japanese Inn* (New York: Random House, 1961), pp. 323, 46.

governing fraternization, the difficulties of travel in a country where Americans could neither read nor speak the language, and the war-shattered state of Japan itself were not conducive to extensive tourism and study. And many soldiers were simply not interested in exploring another dimension of their erstwhile enemy. John Gunther, when he visited Japan in 1950, reported that "one day we went to the Kabuki theater. . . . The theater was jammed; it holds 2,500 people; we were the only Americans there, though the Kabuki is not off limits." He himself added, however, "The Japanese audience moans, howls, and shrieks as the fantastic pantomime proceeds; we thought we were seated among savages."[2]

Zen and Flower Arranging

Tourism proper and the widespread appreciation of Japanese culture did not begin to blossom until the end of the occupation (28 April 1952). A bare four months later, *Holiday* magazine ran a long article by James Michener which issued the invitation: "For the past seven years Americans have occupied Japan as victors. Their occupation has been just and gentle, reflecting credit on each nation; but from now on Americans who visit Japan will do so as guests of a sovereign country. If you are one of the lucky ones, you will find in Japan a land of exquisite beauty and a people dedicated to its cultivation." Michener's article is a sensitive and sensible tour d'horizon. He describes Tokyo and Kyoto, Japanese foods, the Japanese bath, Japanese manners; he even tells the story of the forty-seven *rōnin* (also recounted by Lafcadio Hearn and Ruth Benedict, and later by Oliver Statler and countless others). But Michener's chief emphasis is on the artistic aspects of Japanese culture: "No other nation is so profoundly dedicated to art. Mrs. Sato's lunch is a masterpiece. Her daughters' kimonos were designed by skilled artists. Japanese books are the most artistically printed in the world. Japanese gardens are things of rare beauty and even the most ordinary implements of living are apt to be as lovely as Grecian urns."[3]

About the same time as Michener's article, from June until December 1952, Elizabeth Gray Vining's *Windows for the Crown Prince*

---

[2] John Gunther, *The Riddle of MacArthur* (New York: Harper & Brothers, 1951), p. 86.

[3] James A. Michener, "Japan," *Holiday*, August 1952, p. 32.

was on the best-seller list. Although much of the book's fascination for Americans lay in her intimate acquaintance with the Japanese emperor and his family, she too did her share in promoting Japanese culture. She described her flower-arranging lessons, *gagaku* court music, imperial duck-netting, the temples and gardens of Kyoto, and much more. Both she and Gunther (in his best seller *The Riddle of MacArthur,* published in 1951) sang the praises of the Tawaraya, a Japanese-style hotel in Kyoto, so that it soon became almost exclusively patronized by Americans, just as Statler's *Japanese Inn* was to make the Minaguchi-ya a fashionable tourist spot during the 1960s.

It was also during the early 1950s that Japan first began to export some of her cultural attractions, partly in order to stimulate tourism. In December 1951, the film *Rashomon* opened in New York after having won the grand prize at the Venice Film Festival the previous autumn. Bosley Crowther, the *New York Times* movie critic, praised its camera work, acting, and "hypnotic power," although he seemed a bit baffled by "an artistic achievement of such distinct and exotic character that it is difficult to estimate it alongside conventional story films." [4] *Ugetsu,* which he reviewed on 8 September 1954, after its New York premiere, he also judged "hard for American audiences to comprehend . . . for both the theme and the style of exposition . . . have a strangely obscure, inferential, almost studiedly perplexing quality." [5] But Crowther was completely won over by the beautiful *Gate of Hell,* which won the Cannes Film Festival's grand prize in the spring of 1954 and made its appearance in New York in December of that year. He not only praised its color—"of a richness and harmony that matches that of any film we've ever seen"—but was caught up by its story and atmosphere. "It is hard to convey in simple language the moving qualities of this lovely film. . . . The secret, perhaps, of its rare excitement is the subtlety with which it blends a subterranean flood of hot emotions with the most magnificent flow of surface serenity. . . . The very essence of ancient Japanese culture is rendered a tangible stimulant in this film." [6] Consul General Jun Tsuchiya, who attended and spoke at the New York opening of *Gate of Hell,* took a more practical line: "To me, it is entirely conceivable that the export of superior films will greatly help my country in its present unremitting struggle to become self-sufficient, to

---

[4] *New York Times,* 27 December 1951, p. 18.

[5] *New York Times,* 8 September 1954, p. 40.

[6] *New York Times,* 14 December 1954, p. 45.

rely on trade, not aid." He said he expected that the export of such films would also stimulate tours and travel to Japan.[7]

In addition to Japanese films, the year 1954 brought New Yorkers the Azuma Kabuki Dancers—the first time live Kabuki had been seen in the United States—and a replica of a sixteenth-century Japanese house (a "gift of the Japanese people") on view in the garden of the Museum of Modern Art. The Azuma Kabuki group became a New York sellout attraction and occasioned a cover article in the *Saturday Review of Literature* by the Kabuki scholar Faubion Bowers. Actually, the Kabuki seen in New York was not wholly traditional since Azuma, the group's founder and the daughter of a famous Kabuki actor, took the major female roles herself. In traditional Kabuki, all female roles are enacted by men. Faubion Bowers was careful to explain that these female impersonators, "while leading ordinary conventional lives, playing baseball, and rearing large families, are often idolized by their fans for their exquisite onstage femininity." [8] Nevertheless, Sol Hurok may have judged 1954 America insufficiently prepared to absorb both the strange conventions of Kabuki and the sight of men in drag. Even without the element of men portraying women, the *New York Times* reviewer John Martin—who raved about the costumes, music, acting, and dancing—noted that, "though there is assuredly no lack of vigor, everything is characterized by delicacy and proportion." [9]

The Japanese house at the Museum of Modern Art was praised in almost identical terms. The Sunday *New York Times Magazine* devoted several pages of commentary and photos to the house on the day of its opening to the public, 20 June 1954, particularly noting that "the empty rooms have a luxury of space and an uncluttered serenity." This led one reader to write in that, while she admired the restful, "uncluttered look," she wondered whether life was not of its very nature full of clutter, prompting yet another New Yorker to respond: "A Huzzah! for Mrs. Helen Gross for her letter . . . and a resounding boo for all those who scream with delight over that 'uncluttered' Japanese house at the Museum of Modern Art. I . . . spent an uncomfortable time last winter dining and sleeping in a Japanese inn that was just as uncluttered and unlivable. . . . I suggest some of your uncluttered, airy

---

[7] Ibid.

[8] Faubion Bowers, "Concerning Kabuki," *Saturday Review of Literature,* 27 February 1954, p. 25.

[9] *New York Times,* 28 February 1954, section 2, p. 4.

readers and writers try sleeping on the floor in an uncluttered, drafty room in a 20-degree January night."[10] Clearly, not everyone was instantaneously captivated by Japanese housing, although the *New York Times Magazine* was no doubt correct in pointing out that "despite its exotic, far-away quality, the house has . . . a unique relevance to modern Western architecture. The flexible, open plan, the closely related indoor and outdoor areas, the structural elements emphasized as decorative, are all devices common to our own architecture today."

Still another cultural export of Japan during the mid-1950s was Zen. In one sense, it is probably accurate to say that Zen had a rather limited appeal—primarily on college campuses, which a decade later turned to drugs and Indian mysticism, and among members of the Beat Generation such as Jack Kerouac, Allen Ginsberg, and Gary Snyder. But Zen philosophy also influenced the later work of J. D. Salinger—for example, his two stories "Franny" and "Zooey," which first appeared in the *New Yorker* in 1955 and 1957, and which went on to become a best-selling book in 1961. And Zen had two indefatigable popularizers who became known to the general public, Daisetz Suzuki and Alan Watts. Suzuki, who was Japanese-born but then living and lecturing in the United States, was the subject of a highly flattering profile in the 31 August 1957, issue of the *New Yorker*. Elizabeth Gray Vining, who had first met him in 1947 in Japan, also devoted a chapter of her 1960 book, *Return to Japan,* to Suzuki and Zen in which she wrote about him: "One knew at once that he had had the experience called *satori,* that breaking through the mind barrier into the wholeness of understanding which is the goal of the Zen devotee. Light and love seemed to stream from him; his gentleness was clothed in simplicity, his austerity touched with humor."[11] Alan Watts, meanwhile, was lecturing about Zen on television and radio, as well as writing some two dozen books to explain Zen to Americans. Watts was canonized in the 21 April 1961 issue of *Life,* which devoted four pages of text and photos to him and his works.

The Martial Arts

The late 1950s was also a time when a less precious, more gutsy view of Japanese culture made its first appearance since the war. In 1956,

---

[10] *New York Times Magazine,* 11 July and 18 July 1954.
[11] Elizabeth Gray Vining, *Return to Japan* (New York: J. B. Lippincott, 1960), p. 165.

Kurosawa's film *The Magnificent Seven* was first shown in New York. Bosley Crowther compared it to *High Noon,* an apt observation since in 1960 the Japanese film was actually remade as an American western, with gun-slingers replacing the samurai who saved farmers from the depredations of bandits. The year 1957 also brought Americans a return of Mr. Moto, John Marquand's Japanese detective. In 1934, Marquand had published his first Mr. Moto story (the novel *No Hero,* published first in the *Saturday Evening Post* as "Mr. Moto Takes a Hand") after a trip to the Far East to collect local color. Between then and the outbreak of war, Marquand published five more Mr. Moto novels, the last of them *(Last Laugh, Mr. Moto)* serialized in *Collier's* only three months before Pearl Harbor.

Just as the prewar Mr. Moto stories had darkened to conform with the troubled times, so the first postwar novel, *Stopover Tokyo,* paints a rather accurate picture of postoccupation Japan, which Marquand had revisited in 1955, and of American attitudes. The American hero works for the CIA, and the villains are the Russians (or "Commies") who have trained several Americans to work in Japan as spies. These Russian-trained spies are plotting to kill a liberal Japanese politician and pin it on the Americans, thereby hoping to provoke anti-American riots. The ultimate aim of the villains is to move Japan into the Communist camp. As the American CIA chief says to the hero, "Frankly, I wouldn't say that Japan is very firmly in the camp of the freedom-loving nations. Why should it be? Well, we lost China, and God help us if Japan goes Communist. We'll be in the grinders then. . . ." Says Mr. Moto to the hero, "I am being frank. . . . There are groups here on the Left, and on the Right, too, so anxious to arouse feelings against America. And the plain Japanese man can change so quickly." *Stopover Tokyo* has a gloomy, cold-war atmosphere, not unlike that of *The Spy Who Came in From the Cold;* spies kill each other quietly so that the average citizen can sleep a little more safely in his bed. Mr. Moto and his American counterpart are professionals who can joke about their wartime work, which made them temporary enemies: " 'In Burma, Mr. Rhyce . . . we had your name on file. Japanese linguist, born in Japan. I even had a glimpse of you once at Myitkyna.' Mr. Moto laughed heartily. 'I did not speak because I was moving the other way.' " [12]

---

12 John Marquand, *Stopover Tokyo* (Boston: Little, Brown, & Co., 1957), pp. 22, 228, 219-20.

Marquand caught a political mood and invented a plot for it that a few years later was transmuted into reality: In October 1960, the socialist leader Asanuma was stabbed to death by a right-wing student and earlier that year riots over the renegotiation of the Japanese-American Security Treaty led to the cancellation of a planned visit to Japan by President Eisenhower. Americans were temporarily shocked and dismayed by these events, just as they were a decade later by the grisly ritual suicide of Yukio Mishima. Newspapers worried anew over the Japanese penchant for violence and fanaticism and speculated about the relative strengths of the militant political left and right. But basically, these events had a short half-life in America's consciousness. Six months after John F. Kennedy was elected President, Edwin O. Reischauer arrived in Japan as the new U.S. ambassador, vowing to reopen "the broken dialogue with Japan"; he implied that problems between the two countries were as much America's fault as Japan's and pledged himself to improve "understanding" between the two nations. Even aside from Reischauer's efforts, the cold war was loosening its grip on American thinking and there was a growing sense that Japan had to be judged on its own terms and not merely as our former protégé. The change in American outlook is palpable if one compares, for example, Elizabeth Gray Vining's *Windows for the Crown Prince,* published in 1952, with her *Return to Japan,* published in 1960. Whereas in the first book she often sounds sanctimonious and full of talk about the need to imbue the Japanese people (and particularly Prince Akihito) with the values of democracy and individualism, her second book is much more that of someone enjoying and trying to understand the Japaneseness of Japan. It is the book not of a teacher, but of a tourist.

Tourism and Japanese Inns

The decade of the 1960s was, par excellence, the period of American tourism to Japan (see Table 2). In 1961 the number of American visitors for the first time passed 100,000 a year, and by 1970 it had passed 300,000. The period embraced the first Olympics to be held in Japan (or in any Asian country, for that matter), and the first Japanese-based world's fair. Japan presented an extraordinarily attractive visage to foreigners during this decade. The grinding hardships of the immediate postwar years were over and life was becoming somewhat more comfortable—particularly for the tourist taking advantage of a favorable

Table 2

AMERICAN VISITORS TO JAPAN (INCLUDING TOURISTS, STUDENTS, AND BUSINESSMEN, BUT NOT IN-TRANSIT VISITORS)

Year	Number of Visitors	Year	Number of Visitors
1951	6,600	1962	114,497
1952	13,746	1963	129,814
1953	18,154	1964	136,446
1954	23,157	1965	150,200
1955	28,194	1966	173,500
1956	35,593	1967	187,373
1957	41,041	1968	199,581
1958	53,924	1969	255,663
1959	71,585	1970	315,211
1960	85,881	1971	271,029
1961	103,150	1972	315,897

Source: Government of Japan, Ministry of Transportation (Tourist Industry Bureau) and Ministry of Justice. There is no single series of tourism figures for these years, but where there were discrepancies the lower figure was chosen.

exchange rate. Japan was rapidly becoming a modern, industrialized nation, but not so rapidly that the old culture could not still be seen and savored. It was, in short, a perfect time to visit Zen temples and gardens, to buy lacquerware and mingei pottery, and also to travel in brand-new "bullet" trains and air-conditioned taxis, and buy cameras and watches. In October 1961, when *Holiday* magazine devoted an entire issue to Japan, it stressed precisely this exotic and appealing mixture of old and new. The editors noted, "Of all the countries to which *Holiday* has devoted special issues, none has been more difficult to understand, more demanding of patience, than Japan. It *is* remote from our comprehension, it *is* baffling, it *is* topsy-turvy to the eye and mind. Japan presents us with an overwhelming double image, one face turned to its classical past, the other preoccupied with the present and with Western ways of thinking, behaving, working." Unfortunately, some people seemed to expect that this double image would persist unchanged forever. But just as it has cynically been said that in the United States an integrated neighborhood is merely one that is in transit between being all-white and all-black, so one suspects that Japan during the 1960s was in transit between being a still partly traditional Asian

84

nation and a fully westernized world power. And the more Japan moved in the latter direction, the less most tourists liked it.

Four cartoons published in the 21 October 1969 *Look* magazine illustrate some of the ambivalent feelings of Americans toward Japan during the 1960s. The cartoons comment on the crass response of American tourists to Japanese architecture, on the Japanese student riots of the 1960s, on the cramped living conditions in Japan, and on the strange mixture of old and new in the culture. By contrast, a cartoon dating from the mid-1970s shows that Japanese movies were no longer an incomprehensible or avant-garde art form in the United States, but something that had filtered down to a large segment of the population.

A plethora of tourist-oriented books about Japan was published during the 1960s; for a while it seemed as if everyone who had been there for even a brief period of time (David Riesman's voluminous *Conversations in Japan* is based on a two-month visit) wanted to tell the world about it. The books ranged from the arty (Fosco Maraini's *Meeting with Japan,* Sacheverell Sitwell's *The Bridge of the Brocade Sash*) to the journalistic (Alexander Campbell's *The Heart of Japan,* Richard Halloran, *Japan: Images and Realities*) to the philosophical (Arthur Koestler's *The Lotus and the Robot*) to the unclassifiable (my personal favorite for this period, Bernard Rudofsky's *The Kimono Mind*). But none of these books was an American best seller (although Maraini's book came close). The one book that was a best seller for half a year in 1961 and that continued to sell to tourists going to Japan in subsequent years was Oliver Statler's *Japanese Inn.*

One is tempted to call *Japanese Inn* a "deserved" best seller because it is a well-researched, intelligently conceived, and charmingly executed book that still reads well today. At the same time, it is doubtful that it would be a best seller if it were published today, and Statler has written other, equally good books about Japan since 1961 that have disappeared without a trace. *Japanese Inn* was obviously timely. It coincided with the general American public's curiosity about Japan and the tourists' desire to read something about Japan before they went there. *Japanese Inn* satisfied both these audiences because it was not a pure travelog—a recitation of cities, scenes, and impressions that is more likely to interest someone who is actually going to these places than the armchair traveler. Instead, *Japanese Inn* is a form of "potted history"—a fictionalized treatment of historical events and cultural developments, set in an actual inn. Statler is frank to admit that most of the connections

"Well, anyway, it keeps the rain out."

Drawing by Dick Oldden

Drawing by Dick Oldden

"Someday, son, all this will be yours."

Drawing by Dick Oldden

Drawing by Dick Oldden

I'll go to a Japanese movie with you only if you promise
you won't do that awful samurai grunting after.

Drawing by William Hamilton; © 1974 Chronicle Publishing Co.

between the inn and the historical figures in his book are invented: "The account of the inn's founding conforms to family legend, but most of the links with historical personalities, all of whom I have tried to present faithfully, are my own invention. This is true up until the time of Prince Saionji: Saionji's relationship to the inn is given as it was." [13] But spurious or not, *Japanese Inn* did not ill serve the thousands of American tourists who spent a pleasant night or two at the Minaguchi-ya dreaming of the shoguns and samurai who had preceded them. It merely catered to and reinforced their more romantic perceptions of Japan.

James Bond in Japan

Three years later, a slightly different but equally exotic vision of Japan was captivating many Americans. Ian Fleming's *You Only Live Twice* is full of shrewd observations about Japan, but inevitably—given its genre—it stresses the elements of violence in the culture. James Bond's archenemy, Ernst Blofeld, has moved to Japan and bought a medieval castle which he has landscaped with poisonous plants, piranha-filled pools, and dangerous sulfur springs. The purpose is to lure the supposedly suicide-prone Japanese to their deaths: "A garden that would be like a deadly fly-trap for human beings, a killing bottle for those who wanted to die. And of course Japan, with the highest suicide statistics in the world, a country with an unquenchable thirst for the bizarre, the cruel, and the terrible, would provide the perfect last refuge for [Blofeld]." [14] In order to kill Blofeld, Bond is given a short course in *ninjutsu* by his Japanese police contact, Tiger Tanaka (who had hoped to be a kamikaze pilot during the war): "My agents are trained in one of the arts most dreaded in Japan—*ninjutsu,* which is, literally, the art of stealth or invisibility. All the men you will see have already graduated in at least ten of the eighteen martial arts of *bushido,* or 'way of the warrior,' and they are now learning to be *ninja,* or 'stealers-in,' which has for centuries been part of the basic training of spies and assassins

---

13 Statler, *Japanese Inn,* p. 363.

14 Ian Fleming, *You Only Live Twice* (New York: Signet Books, 1965), p. 99. Actually, in 1964 Japan ranked tenth in terms of frequency of suicide, after West Berlin, Hungary, Austria, Denmark, Czechoslovakia, West Germany, Finland, Sweden, and Switzerland. See George De Vos, *Socialization for Achievement* (Berkeley: University of California Press, 1973), p. 455.

and saboteurs." [15] At the same time, Fleming puts down some of the treasured peaceful arts of Japan:

> The geisha party had been going on for two hours, and Bond's jaws were aching with the unending smiles and polite repartee. Far from being entertained by the geisha, or bewitched by the inscrutable discords issuing from the catskin-covered box of the three-stringed *samisen,* Bond had found himself having to try desperately to make the party go. . . . Dikko Henderson had warned him that geisha parties were more or less the equivalent, for a foreigner, of trying to entertain a lot of unknown children in a nursery with a strict governess, the madame looking on.[16]

It all seems a far cry from Michener's *Sayonara* until one meets Bond's abalone-diving girlfriend Kissy Suzuki and we are once again face to face with the perfect Japanese woman: loyal, brave, selfless.

If one were to try to generalize about popular American impressions of Japanese culture from Michener to Fleming—that is, from 1954 to 1964—there would be a number of constants: the charm of Japanese women, the beauty of the landscape, and the refinement of many of the traditional arts. One would also have to note some changes. There seems to have been a progression in American interest from some of the more obvious features of traditional Japanese culture—flower-arranging, Kabuki, woodblock prints—to some of the more subtle aspects—Zen, mingei pottery, Japanese gardens—to, finally, a renewed interest in some of its more martial aspects—akido and kendo, samurai movies, ritual suicide. Perhaps this progression of images is, in fact, a rather healthy sign of an increasing American ability to come to terms with Japanese culture in all its dimensions. In the immediately postwar years Americans may have feminized Japanese society partly because they wanted to repress their wartime memories. They were aided in their efforts by the fact that they came as conquerors and Japanese men tried to keep a low profile. In recent years, a more masculine image of Japan is being projected, both in the traditional culture and in the more mundane efforts of Japan's assertive businessmen. It would be a pity if, as in the prewar period, the masculine, aggressive image once more came to blot out the soft, feminine one; however, the recombining of yin and yang in a balanced whole is all to the good.

---

[15] Fleming, *You Only Live Twice,* p. 79.
[16] Ibid., p. 11.

Another change in American perceptions of Japanese culture may be more damaging. Americans moved from a period of postwar cultural chauvinism—"gook" food was terrible, the Japanese did everything backwards, Japanese houses and artifacts were too small and fragile—into a period of exoticism when traditional Japanese culture was greatly admired at the expense of modernity. The result is that today many Americans, when asked about Japanese culture, complain bitterly that it has disappeared or been "spoiled." Pollution, high prices, the automobile, modern apartment houses—all these cause some Americans (and not a few Japanese) to say that Japanese culture is dead or dying.

There is no answer to this line of argument. Pollution, prices, the number of automobiles and apartment houses have all increased in Japan since the 1950s, and if these are not compatible with one's definition of culture then Japanese culture is indeed on the decline. Even those willing to admit that a modern industrialized society may still have a culture, can argue that it no longer pleases them, and such attitudes are likely to have an effect on future rates of tourism to Japan. At the same time, for every disenchanted Japanophile, a new enthusiast seems to be born. One sees this best in the reminiscences of old Japan-hands of various vintages. "Japan isn't the same any more," a fortyish professor or businessman will say, "you should have seen it in the fifties, when I first went there." An older man, whose memories go back to Japan in the early thirties, may keep still, knowing that no one in the room can share his memories. Meanwhile, someone who first saw Japan in the 1960s will review his experiences critically and wonder why he had such a good time. And a young student about to go to Japan in the 1970s will set out with trepidation, perhaps to discover that all and none of them are right: Japanese culture is a changing, living thing and perceptions of it must necessarily change accordingly.

7

The Business Nexus

All of the American stereotypes with regard to Japan have undergone changes over the years—for example, our views of the Japanese at war, of our own A-bombing of Hiroshima, and of Japanese culture—but in no area have the stereotypes changed more rapidly than in the field of business. In 1949, as we have seen, the *Saturday Evening Post* was attacking the occupation by arguing that "We're Giving Japan Democracy, but She Can't Earn Her Living." In May 1951, shortly before the end of the occupation, *Fortune* asked, "Can Japan Pay Her Own Way?" and answered the question in only a guardedly optimistic fashion. In 1954 in an article entitled "Japan: Help Needed," *Fortune* was still worrying about Japan's dwindling foreign exchange because her imports were far exceeding exports. Yet two years later U.S. textile manufacturers were already calling for import quotas on Japanese-made textiles, and by 1957 *Fortune* was trumpeting that "defeated in war, stripped of colonies, never rich in resources, Japan has reemerged as the foremost industrial power in Asia." [1]

As American attitudes toward Japan's economic viability changed, so also did the attitudes toward Japanese products themselves. In the immediate postwar period, Americans regarded Japanese-made items as cheaply but shoddily made. In 1949, *Business Week* reported that "war and occupation have not changed Japan's traditional tendency to dump poor-quality products on world markets. American engineers here are convinced of this after rejecting thousands of dollars worth of Japanese manufactures that didn't even come close to contract specifications." [2]

---

[1] John Davenport, "In Japan It's 'Jimmu Keiki,' " *Fortune,* July 1957, p. 107.

[2] *Business Week,* 17 December 1949, p. 106.

The article goes on to give details about a $300,000 shipment of transformers of which only 1 percent were usable, and a $700,000 shipment of radio equipment for Korea of which only one-seventh of the units worked. When an official of the Wireless Communication Equipment Industrial Association of Japan tried to answer some of these charges, *Business Week* in effect ridiculed Japanese business still further by printing the letter without editorial changes. Written in somewhat quaint English, the letter tried to explain that not all the defects could be blamed on the manufacturers: "a part of the shipments were carried by trucks all the criggy way to Seoul, where the goods were hurled down in such a senseless way, thus subsequently caused considerable damages after all. While the rest of the shipment were left untouched outside the godowns over six months, on some of which naturally caused electrical inefficiencies, and there found those still practically workable is nothing but two-thirds of all." [3]

Nonetheless, only two years later, in mid-1951, Japanese manufacturers held a successful eighteen-day trade fair in Seattle, where they displayed 8,000 items ranging from knickknacks, to cultured pearls, bicycles, canned fish, and sewing machines. *Business Week* reported that "at first buyers were dubious about the quality of Japan's products. But now, with the fair over, the consensus is that there's been real improvement over prewar. Some items—like cameras, binoculars, sewing machines—were felt to be right up to U.S. standards." [4] In 1957, *Business Week* accorded Nikon and Canon an even higher accolade when it ranked their products "in the same category as German cameras." [5] It also pointed out that Japanese manufacturers were beginning to appeal to the "quality market" in a number of other fields, and it quoted one American importer who predicted "a whole new group of Japanese products, based on Japan's great artistic traditions, can change U.S. homes as much as the Scandinavian-modern designs did in the 1930s and the 1940s." [6] This is, of course, precisely what happened.

In a general way, it is clear that the postwar American image of the Japanese economy changed, in accordance with actual changes in Japan, from one of great weakness to one of great strength. One way to illustrate this is with several cartoons. The first, from the 30 Septem-

---

[3] Ibid., 8 April 1950, p. 66.
[4] Ibid., 7 July 1951, p. 148.
[5] Ibid., 7 September 1957, p. 158.
[6] Ibid., 24 September 1955, p. 150.

ber 1945 *New York Times Magazine,* pokes fun at the Japanese willingness to copy any foreign product and produce it more cheaply than the original. The second, dating from 1974, pokes fun not at the Japanese but at Americans trying to balance their consumer interest in a Japanese car against their ecological concern for whales, which were then being over-hunted by the Japanese whaling industry. The third, also from the mid-1970s, comments wryly on the strength of the Japanese economy by depicting its investors, rather than Americans, as international pace-setters.

At the same time that Americans were changing their impressions of the Japanese economy, their impressions of Japanese products were changing. They stopped thinking of them as cheap, shoddy, and gimcrack, and began to regard them as highly reliable, precision-made, and well designed. By the 1970s, many Americans were deliberately buying Japanese-made radios, television sets, and automobiles because they believed them to be *better* than comparable American-made items, and many more Americans were buying Japanese-made products without knowing their country of origin because they were sold under American brand names. When President Ford visited Japan in November 1974, he presented a group of Japanese Diet members with portable cassette recorders which turned out, underneath their American trade mark, to be discreetly marked "Made in Japan." [7]

American Hostility toward Japanese Business

But despite the postwar trend of favorable American attitudes toward Japanese business, some much harsher images reappear with startling regularity. The American convictions that the Japanese undersell other nations because their wages are low, that they steal patents, that they dump products on foreign markets in order to swamp competitors, and that they are ruthless in their pursuit of trade, all surface whenever the balance of trade between the United States and Japan becomes even slightly skewed in favor of Japan. The traditional Japanese response is to turn the other cheek, to adopt a low profile and, for example, put voluntary quotas on exports in order to avoid having the United States impose quotas and tariffs. But even Japanese efforts to bow to U.S. demands are frequently criticized as being "insincere" or

---

[7] *Newsweek,* 2 December 1974, p. 26.

"Japanese manufacturers competent for making atomic bomb
more cheaper, saving American gentleman many dollars. Yes please?"

Reprinted with permission from the New York Times Magazine

But aren't you afraid if we buy a Japanese car we'll be letting
down the whales?

Drawing by William Hamilton; © 1974 Chronicle Publishing Co.

"Your race horses, your wines, your philanthropy to Ivy League colleges, your works of art—really, Teddy, you're practically Japanese."

Drawing by William Hamilton; © 1973 The **New Yorker** Magazine, Inc.

"devious." One senses, in these reactions of the American business community, a transmutation of wartime prejudices, perhaps conditioned by the fact that many present-day middle-aged businessmen were young soldiers in the Pacific during World War II. Even the language in which Japanese trade is described often echoes wartime terminology. For example, in September 1970, *Fortune* magazine—under a headline reading "How the Japanese Mount that Export Blitz: a powerful government-business complex dubbed 'Japan Inc.' Its weapons include cartels, price cutting, and unbounded patriotic zeal"—wrote: "To hard-pressed competitors around the world, Japan's export drive is taking on the overtones of a relentless conspiracy to invade and dominate every vital international market."

It is, of course, important to distinguish between the feelings of relatively small, if vocal, pressure groups of businessmen and the mass of American consumers. But even among consumers there are some disquieting signs that favorable opinions about Japanese goods are not strongly held. In 1959, when Japanese-American trade was roughly balanced at about $1 billion in each direction (in 1973 it was again roughly in balance, but this time at $9 billion in each direction), a survey found that a third of the Americans interviewed opposed more trade with Japan. Moreover, although Japan was then selling the United States $8.6 million in photographic equipment, $28.2 million worth of electrical goods (including radios, shavers, and the like), and $11.8 million worth of scientific and professional instruments, most Americans still thought of Japan as a producer of toys and ceramics. Seventy-eight percent also thought that the quality of Japanese items was below that of things made in the United States.[8] Presumably, today the American public would more readily associate the name of Japan with high-quality products such as radios, tape recorders, motorcycles, and automobiles. But the Japanese fear that popular American attitudes might turn rapidly against even these admired products if a prolonged recession in the United States put many automobile and electronics workers out of jobs.

Japanese Efforts to Combat Hostility

The volatile nature of the American response to Japanese goods has led many Japanese businesses to hire American public relations firms to tell them how to improve their overseas image. Discussions have been

---

[8] *Business Week,* 19 September 1959, p. 150.

organized between Japanese and American businessmen and scholars to "improve communication," and Japanese enterprises such as Mitsubishi, Sumitomo, and Toyota have recently begun to endow chairs for Japanese studies at major American universities and to sponsor scholarships for American students in the somewhat naive belief that Americans expect a company to have a "social role." It is true, of course, that major American firms occasionally underwrite prestigious noncommercial television programs, donate money to opera and ballet companies, or establish nonprofit foundations. Management generally views such largesse as a valuable tax write-off that may yield some side-benefits in terms of "good public relations." But it seems doubtful that the existence of the Ford Foundation makes people any better disposed toward the Ford Motor Company, or that the Johnson Foundation influences housewives trying to decide between Johnson's and some other brand of floor wax. Similarly, the Mitsubishi chair at Harvard is not likely to have much impact on the sale of Japanese rice-cookers or structural steel in the United States, although it probably cannot do any harm either.

The notion that "improved communication" can enhance the image of Japanese business in the United States is another truism that needs to be examined much more critically. Japanese-American communication—mutual understanding of one another's language, tastes, and life-styles—is probably most advanced in Hawaii, where almost a third of the population is of Japanese descent. And yet nowhere else in the United States has there been so much public criticism of Japanese businesses and investment. Hawaii lies not a great deal further from Japan than it does from the west coast of the United States, and it has become a major tourist attraction for the Japanese. (One reason why tourism statistics about Japanese who have visited the United States are a little misleading is that fully half of those tourists get no further than Hawaii.) Not surprisingly, Japanese businesses have invested heavily in Hawaii, especially in enterprises catering to their own tourists—hotels, golf courses, and department stores. They also tend to staff their newly acquired enterprises predominantly with Japanese-Americans. A 1973 survey of sixty-four Japanese-owned firms in Hawaii found that of 1,744 employees, some 70 percent were of Japanese-American descent.[9]

---

[9] Emily and Robert Heller, *The Economic and Social Impact of Foreign Investment in Hawaii* (Honolulu: University of Hawaii, Economic Research Center, December 1973).

(Japanese-Americans constitute approximately 28 percent of Hawaii's population.)

Other ethnic groups in Hawaii, primarily the native Hawaiians and American-Chinese, resent such employment practices and fear the concentration of Japanese economic power in an industry that is a mainstay of the islands—tourism. By July 1973, it was estimated that 12 percent of the state's hotel rooms—and 35 percent of those in Waikiki—were owned by Japanese interests, as well as three large department stores and some 8,000 acres—0.03 percent of the state's total private land.[10] At the same time, Hawaiian state officials have actively wooed Japanese investors. Senator Hiram Fong himself recently sold some 1,000 acres of land to them, and, beginning in 1971 when the United States had a $2.5 billion trade deficit with Japan, the U.S. Department of Commerce prodded and all but pushed Japan into investing some of its surplus dollars back into the United States. The resulting tensions and hostilities in Hawaii are thus not a product of poor communication between the Japanese and the Americans. Rather, they are caused by the fact that the Japanese have overinvested in Hawaii precisely because they know the place well, and because, having inserted themselves into the delicately balanced Hawaiian racial situation, they are suspected of tipping the scales in the direction of the Japanese-American element of the population. The Japanese did not face this sort of opposition when they took over an aircraft company in Texas, opened a soy sauce plant in Wisconsin, or started a zipper factory in Georgia.[11]

The Overall Success Story

A somewhat more detailed look at American attitudes toward Japanese business reveals that they have fluctuated over the years more or less in accordance with the nature, quality, and size of that business. Up until the end of the occupation, there was considerable doubt about the quality of Japanese goods, although this rapidly disappeared when the newly independent Japanese government began to allow exporters to set up trade associations and began a rigid program of quality controls for exports. In 1953, *Business Week* wrote an article full of admiration for "Japan's effort to rebuild its U.S. markets . . . a dogged, unobtrusive

---

[10] *Honolulu Advertiser,* 16 July 1973.

[11] Wesley Pruden, "The Japanese Have Landed," *National Observer,* 10 November 1973, p. 1.

business operation—more businesslike than it ever was before the war." [12] In 1954, the magazine reported that "The U.S. has decided to go all out to bring Japan into the General Agreement on Tariffs and Trade (GATT), the free world trading community, as a full member." It acknowledged that Europe and the Commonwealth were fearful of Japanese competition, and that some U.S. industries were also highly vulnerable, but it argued that under GATT Japan's entry into foreign markets would be spread across the free world. At that time there was a good deal of concern about keeping the Japanese economy healthy so that it would not be forced into the orbit of Communist China. Already in 1953, *Business Week* reported that Sumitomo Chemical was operating at only 60 percent of capacity and was "straining at the bit for more sales." [13]

The year 1955 was the first postwar year when Japanese-U.S. trade passed its prewar record (see Table 3). American stores were carrying Japanese toys, cameras, chinaware, sewing machines, furniture, ladies' blouses, cashmere sweaters, silks, Christmas ornaments, and pearls, and Japan was also exporting plywood, tuna, and cotton cloth. As a result of the GATT agreements, the United States had made tariff concessions on imports of cotton cloth, chinaware, toys, and Christmas decorations; but California fishing interests demanded a duty on Japanese tuna, and there was also a great deal of pressure for tariffs on such things as "the notorious dollar blouse." Japanese market researchers, it seems, had determined that there would be a large demand for a simple cotton blouse that could be sold across the United States for $1, and to the consternation of American manufacturers, more than a million orders were in fact placed. *Business Week* and other economic writers were sympathetic to Japan and pointed out that it was the largest single market for American raw cotton: in 1955, Japan bought some 647,000 bales, 25 percent of the total the United States exported.[14] Nevertheless, in early January 1957, Japan yielded to the pressures of U.S. textile manufacturers and placed a voluntary quota on its shipments of textiles to the United States.

During the first week of November 1961, a cabinet-level U.S.-Japan Committee on Trade and Economic Affairs met at Hakone, but there

---

[12] *Business Week,* 6 June 1953, p. 144.

[13] Ibid., 25 April 1953, p. 161.

[14] D. L. Cohn, "Southern Cotton and Japan," *Atlantic Monthly,* August 1956, p. 55; and *Business Week,* 24 September 1955.

Table 3

JAPANESE-U.S. TRADE
(\$ millions)

Year	Japanese Imports from the United States	Japanese Exports to the United States
1952	768.3	234.3
1953	759.7	233.9
1954	848.7	282.6
1955	773.9	456.2
1956	1,067.2	550.4
1957	1,623.1	604.5
1958	1,956.1	690.7
1959	1,115.6	1,046.6
1960	1,553.5	1,101.6
1961	2,095.8	1,066.9
1962	1,809.0	1,400.2
1963	2,077.3	1,506.9
1964	2,336.0	1,841.6
1965	2,366.1	2,479.2
1966	2,657.7	2,969.5
1967	3,212.1	3,012.0
1968	3,527.4	4,086.5
1969	4,089.9	4,957.8
1970	5,559.6	5,939.8
1971	4,977.9	7,495.3
1972	5,851.6	8,847.7
1973	9,269.6	9,448.7
1974	12,700.0	12,800.0

Source: Japanese government, Ministry of International Trade and Industry.

was not much agreement between the two countries about their growing trade gap. (Japan was then importing \$1 billion worth of goods more than it was exporting to the United States.) Japan wanted restrictions on Japanese exports to the United States relaxed, whereas the United States wanted the Japanese "to broaden the base of their international trade with other countries of Asia and with Europe," despite the fact that a number of European countries had (and have) even stiffer barriers against Japanese products. Nevertheless, the Japanese in effect succeeded in achieving both of these goals during the 1960s, so that by 1970 it was exporting $19 billion worth of goods worldwide, $5 billion of it to the United States, which by then had a trade deficit with Japan.

The 1960s was a period of tremendous economic growth for Japan—growth so rapid that many of us tend to forget how recent some of Japan's industrial strength is. For example, Honda and Yamaha only began to sell motorcycles in the United States in 1960; yet in 1966, Honda, Yamaha, and Suzuki between them sold approximately 400,000 motorcycles in the United States, 85 percent of the U.S. sales.[15] Japan did not begin producing passenger automobiles until the late 1950s, and then its production went exclusively for taxis and rental car companies in Japan. Not until 1964 did Toyota ship fifty Coronas to the United States to test consumer reactions. In 1974, it sold American consumers 238,135 cars (and this was a drop of 51,000 from 1973's sales).

It was only in the late 1960s that some of the biggest Japanese export brands—Sony, Seiko, Datsun—became well known to American consumers. Even then, many products were so skillfully named to suit the American market—for example, Panasonic, National, Pioneer—or sold under the brand names of Sears, Montgomery Ward, and J. C. Penney, that many buyers did not know they were purchasing Japanese-made goods. Advertising campaigns were also well designed for American tastes: the Mazda campaign to publicize its rotary engine, Sony's slogan "A Sony of my owny," and Kawasaki's exceedingly vulgar but effective "Get something really exciting between your legs" are only a few examples that come to mind. I suspect that it is here, in the marketing of Japanese products, rather than in the communication styles of Japanese executives, that a little "Americanization" has paid large dividends.

At the same time, the high quality of Japanese products satisfied customers. When, in 1970, the United States's growing trade deficit with Japan once again began to produce a clamor among American manufacturers for tariff barriers, even the normally jingoistic *Time* magazine wrote in a cover story that "the solution does not lie in appeasing protectionist sentiment. Apart from the economic and political implications of business isolationism, the interests of the consumer should rule, and [the] Japanese are giving consumers quality products at reasonable prices." [16] And in an equally sympathetic special report called "Japan's Remarkable Industrial Machine," *Business Week* pointed out that "the

---

[15] *Business Week,* 12 November 1966, p. 140.
[16] *Time,* 10 May 1971, p. 88.

reason for Japan's competitive clout is not low wages any more, but a combination of factors including modern plants, rising labor productivity, and efficient management." [17]

In 1971, the United States did force an upward revaluation of the yen in order to correct its trade imbalance with Japan. The Japanese were fearful that the sudden increase in the cost of their exports would lead to a dramatic drop in sales, but this proved not to be the case. Japanese exports to the United States continued to climb to an all-time high of $12.8 billion during 1974. It is, of course, possible that this volume of trade will decline somewhat in 1975 and 1976 due to the general recession being experienced in the United States, and it is almost certain that balance-of-payments problems will continue to be aggravated by the high price of Middle Eastern oil. Japan had a trade surplus of approximately $1 billion with the United States in 1974, but an overall balance-of-payments deficit of $6.8 billion, almost all of it caused by skyrocketing oil prices. But these difficulties should not obscure the fact that Japanese business was the *wunderkind* of the postwar world, and that the American public has been, by and large, an eager and admiring consumer of its many offerings.

---

[17] *Business Week,* 7 March 1970, p. 60.

8
Conclusion

What, in the final analysis, do all of these various impressions add up to? In the last thirty-five years Americans have thought of the Japanese as warlike and cruel, as charming and artistic, as business-oriented and clever. We have been hostile toward the Japanese; remorseful over Hiroshima; condescending, admiring, wary, irritated, and baffled in the face of Japanese culture. To some extent all of these attitudes coexist in the United States, since different groups of Americans are drawing upon different experiences with Japan to form their stereotypes. Many of the stereotypes have their roots in specific events so that one cannot call them entirely erroneous, although like all stereotypes they tend to be one-dimensional. One purpose of this study is to promote a more stereoscopic vision of Japan by summarizing and analyzing some of the events that have molded American opinions during the last thirty-five years.

The Limitations of National Character

Another purpose of this study is to argue that national stereotypes are based on specific impressions of people and events rather than on something immutable known as national character. If the latter were true, we would be at a loss to explain the frequent and rapid changes that American perceptions of the Japanese have undergone. In the first chapter, I described how the concept of national character was, in fact, developed during World War II as a curious amalgam of Freudian insights, anthropological methods developed in the study of small, primitive tribes, and the necessity of conducting psychological warfare against our enemies. The language of national character studies was never very

109

exact, and its hypotheses have frequently been dismissed as tautological. Since World War II, one social scientist, Anthony Wallace, has demonstrated that in two different societies only between 28 and 37 percent of the adult populations possessed the "modal personalities" of those cultures (where modal personality was defined in terms of twenty-one parameters, which still left a great deal of room for diversity in other personality traits).[1] Another social scientist, Alex Inkeles, has presented some very persuasive statistics demonstrating that the perceptions and values of certain social groups—for example, bureaucrats and factory workers—resemble one another cross-culturally more than they resemble those of other groups in their own society. In other words, a factory worker in the United States may have more in common with a factory worker in Japan than with an American banker, professor, or farmhand.[2] If this is so, then the concept of national character has been dealt a formidable blow.

Scholars who nevertheless cling to the notion of national character tend to phrase their conclusions impressionistically and, in the case of Japan, frequently invoke rapid change, cultural lag, and even "the mysterious East" to gloss over the variety of personality types and life styles that actually exist in modern Japan. A recent example of this sort of approach to Japanese national character was the series of Japanese films shown on American public television stations in early 1975, complete with commentaries by Edwin O. Reischauer. In Chapter 6, I myself discussed the impact made by some of these movies during the late 1950s and early 1960s in promoting a specific *stereotype* of Japan— the travel-poster image of Japan as a land of samurai, geisha, tea ceremonies, and beautiful Zen temples. But there is a great deal of difference between noting that movies may influence one's impressions of a society, and asserting that they provide objective insights into that society and its citizens. The technique of using movies in order to analyze the societies that produced them, of course, goes back to World War II and the beginnings of national character studies. But at that time movies were

---

[1] Anthony Wallace, "The Modal Personality Structure of the Tuscarora Indians as Revealed by the Rorschach Test," *Bulletin,* Bureau of American Ethnology, no. 150; and "Individual Differences and Cultural Uniformities," *American Sociological Review,* vol. 17 (1952), pp. 747-50.

[2] Alex Inkeles, "Industrial Man: The Relation of Status to Experience, Perception, and Value," *American Journal of Sociology,* vol. 66 (July 1960), pp. 1-31; and *Becoming Modern: Individual Change in Six Developing Countries* (Cambridge, Mass.: Harvard University Press, 1974).

used *faute de mieux*—for lack of something better, such as access to the society itself. And, as many critics of national character studies have since pointed out, the use of films was partly responsible for some of the distortions in national character analyses—for example, Ruth Benedict's assumption that the samurai code of ethics *(bushido)* was still functioning in the Japan of the 1930s.

In order to bring the matter closer to home, let us try to imagine a series of films that might be chosen to portray American culture to other nations: *The Grapes of Wrath, Gone With the Wind, The Best Years of Our Lives, High Noon, Intruder in the Dust,* and who knows, perhaps even *The Godfather.* The subjects illustrated by these films include the Civil War, the lawlessness of the Wild West, the Dust Bowl and the Great Depression, race relations, World War II and its aftermath, and gangsters and their ethnic ties. No one would argue that the resulting image of the United States is wholly inaccurate, but it certainly emphasizes the elements of tragedy, violence, and group conflict in American history. Similarly, the Japanese films shown on TV emphasized ritual suicide, swashbuckling samurai, the tragedy of World War II, and the self-abnegation of Japanese women. Interesting, beautiful, and moving as the films themselves may be, they are at best only a partial guide to Japan today. At worst, they tend to reinforce old stereotypes and are, in fact, misleading.

The Situational Approach

It would be better, as I suggested in Chapter 1, to set aside the whole notion of national character as little more than prejudice dressed up in scholarly clothing. Popular novels, movies, and the writings of reporters and businessmen are full enough of prejudice and stereotypic thinking; but they have the excuse of not pretending to be the final word on the subject. Instead, they are products of their time, and they both reflect and help to shape the opinions of their time. It strikes me as more accurate, as well as more hopeful, to assume that national stereotypes are based on immediate impressions of people and events rather than upon some deepseated immutable force known as national character.

One hopeful conclusion that might be drawn from the view that national stereotypes do have their roots in specific events is that Japan and other nations have only to behave well on the international scene in order to be loved and admired by everyone. In other words, handsome is as handsome does. Unfortunately, the matter is not so simple. Cultural contact is a two-way street, and a nation's behavior is inevitably conditioned by the interpretation it places on the actions of other nations. What the United States does, no matter how we ourselves choose to interpret it, is bound to be interpreted differently by others and to have an impact on the behavior of other nations like Japan. In terms of the history of the two nations, for example, Noam Chomsky is at least partly correct when he argues that U.S. efforts to embargo Japan during the 1930s helped to produce anti-American and expansionist sentiments among the Japanese, which in turn helped to inflame Americans still further. Whether this spiral of mutual distrust could have been halted by men of good will, and who should bear the blame for the war that actually followed, are not my concern here—though it is worth pointing out that arguments wholly in favor of one side or the other are always likely to be biased, skewing history in order to make some current political point. (Chomsky's argument is that Japan was not fascist and expansionist in the 1930s, but that the United States was, and is). But spirals of mutual interaction and perception exist today, just as they did in the past, and how these may develop in the future should be of concern to all Americans and Japanese.

One example of the two countries' current interaction can be drawn from the realm of trade. In late 1974, growing unemployment in the United States began to create demands among certain labor unions— chiefly garment workers—that "cheap imports" from other countries be halted or limited. Since Japan was already observing a voluntary quota on textiles, the pickets and television stories focussed primarily on cheap labor in Korea, Brazil, and Mexico. But it would not be difficult to imagine a similar U.S. campaign against Japanese-made cars and electronics. The American reaction is a form of scapegoating—why should consumers be permitted to buy Japanese cars when our own automobile workers are being laid off?—never mind the fact that Japanese workers today earn about the same as American workers and that the Japanese have inflation and labor problems of their own. If American import quotas took hold, one result would be that the Japanese would retaliate with import quotas against American goods. Each country's citizens would come to see the other as the root cause of all its miseries—a situation dangerously reminiscent of the 1930s.

A different example of current interaction and possible misinterpretation lies in the realm of mutual security. Under the terms of the mutual security treaty between Japan and the United States, the United States promises to defend Japan in case of attack by a third power; and since the United States is one of those nations possessing atomic weapons, it effectively shields Japan from nuclear blackmail or from the need to build its own nuclear deterrent. Much as this treaty benefits Japan—for example, in terms of the percentage of its GNP devoted to armaments—there has always been a good deal of criticism by left-wing Japanese of the U.S. bases on their soil. In late 1974, a new and vociferous series of protests erupted in Japan when it was learned that American ships calling at Japanese ports carried unarmed nuclear weapons. The danger of these protests is that Americans may take them seriously and say, in effect, "All right, if you don't want us or our nuclear weapons, we won't bother you. Look to your own interests." Such a development, however, would almost certainly lead to Japanese rearmament; and this, in turn, would have an enormous impact on American (and other nations') perceptions of Japan.

Given the complex relationship between international behavior and the stereotypes of nations, there can be no easy answer to how a particular nation—say, Japan—can maintain a favorable image in the eyes of another nation, such as the United States. Certainly one partial solution is "handsome is as handsome does." Good relations between two countries at the governmental and business levels generally contribute to favorable popular images, while states of war, trade embargoes, or other international tensions promote unflattering popular images. It is interesting, for example, how rapidly American popular opinion became hostile to France—a nation toward which Americans traditionally harbor many favorable sentiments—when de Gaulle vetoed Britain's entry into the Common Market, refused to cooperate with NATO, and began converting France's American dollar holdings into gold. Many American tourists at the time were angry enough to avoid France on their European trips because they did not want to have a part in supporting de Gaulle's policies. Similarly, it is clear that, while the majority of Americans are pro-Israel, Israel's popular image is damaged whenever it conducts a preemptive strike against the Palestinian guerrillas or neighboring Arab countries, or whenever it seems to be the more recalcitrant negotiating partner in the Middle East. With regard to Japan, cries of alarm over Japanese "dumping" and unfair trade practices are heard whenever the American business community feels the pinch of competition. And American faith in Japan's democratic orientation is

113

invariably somewhat shaken by student riots or events such as Mishima's suicide.

Cultivating Multiple Images

If such real events shape popular stereotypes, it is also true that, once stereotypes take hold, they can help to shape international events. It is important, therefore, to ensure that a single unfortunate turn in the international arena (Japanese reluctance to lower tariff barriers against American oranges, say, or American restrictions on soybean exports to Japan) does not begin a spiral of ill will. One way of helping prevent such a spiral is to promote and publicize a multiplicity of stereotypes. In this respect the United States and Japan are very fortunate in having known many favorable images of one another in the course of their relations. For Americans, these include their memories of the occupation, their infatuation with things Japanese during the late 1950s and early 1960s, and their current admiration for Japanese industrial products. Japan is not nearly so fortunate when it comes to its image in the countries of southeast Asia. There, bitter memories of the war linger and are not offset by admiration for Japan's postwar industrial growth, which is often envied and feared.

A multiplicity of images makes it more difficult for a particular stereotype to dominate one nation's perspective on another nation. "The Japanese are sneaky and cruel" may be one residue of World War II. "Yes, but the Japanese are also kind and gentle," is likely to be the response of someone who was there during the occupation. "The Japanese are artistic and nonmaterialistic" may be the impression of a 1960s visitor. "The Japanese are hard-driving businessmen and insensitive to pollution," says the tourist of the 1970s. No doubt each of these images contains, or contained, a kernel of truth; but their multiplicity and impermanence should make us cautious about accepting any one of them as either fixed or wholly accurate. Americans should also be wary of the assertions some Japanese (including Japanese scholars) make about their own culture, since these are often matters of domestic debate—or what the Japanese think Americans want to hear. In the final analysis, Americans would do well to cultivate a permanent suspicion of any sentence that begins "The Japanese are . . . ," with the possible exception of the following: "The Japanese are an interesting and talented people, fully as diverse and capable of change as we credit ourselves with being."